FM 3-31
MCWP 3-40.7

Joint Force Land Component Commander Handbook

U.S. Marine Corps

PCN 143 000097 00

Acknowledgement

This handbook would not have been possible without the guidance and advice of many great individuals. The US Army and US Marines are extremely grateful to the experts who provided their time, expertise, and encouragement. While it is impossible to list everyone, special recognition is given to—

LtCol Mark Triplett, USMC, and MAJ Ken Bowman, USA, co-authors. Special thanks to COL John Bonin, USA; COL Vincent Brooks, USA; COL Rick Steinke, USA; LtCol Michael Bulawka, USMC; LTC Buffy Wilcox, USA; LtCol Andrew Gerke, USMC; LTC Charles Guerry, USA; LTC Charles Maurer, USA; LTC Steve Wallace, USA; MAJ Andrew Curthoys, USA; MAJ Paul Davis, USA; Mr. Bo Bielinski; Mr. Douglas Agee; Mr. William Shugrue; Mr. Terry Patterson; Mr. Steve Leeder; and the members of the Joint Force Land Component Commander's Working Group.

Corrections or suggestions for improvement of this handbook are welcome. Comments should be forwarded to HQ TRADOC, DCSDOC, Joint and Army Doctrine Directorate, Ingalls Road, Building 133, Fort Monroe, Virginia 23651-5000. The telephone number is DSN 680-3892, commercial (757) 788-3892.

FM 3-31
MCWP 3-40.7

Joint Force
Land Component Commander Handbook
(JFLCC)

Contents

i

Preface

SCOPE

This handbook provides guidance for planning and conducting land operations requiring the close coordination of Army forces and Marine Corps forces under the control of a joint force land component commander within a joint operations area. It presents considerations and options that joint force commanders can employ when designating a joint force land component commander and describes the authority and responsibilities of a joint force land component commander.

PURPOSE

This handbook describes guidance for establishing the command relationship based on the joint force commander's concept of operations. It addresses formation, functions, and organization of the joint force land component commander. It also discusses the operational questions of who, what, when, and how of operations in support of major operations or campaigns by a joint force commander. It is not the intent of this handbook to supplant approved joint doctrine; nor is it the intent to restrict the authority of the joint force commander from organizing the force and executing the mission in a manner he deems most appropriate to ensure unity of effort in the accomplishment of the overall mission.

APPLICATION

The guidance in this handbook applies to combatant commanders, sub-joint task forces, and subordinate components of these commands. This handbook is used for guidance and reference only. If conflicts arise between the contents of this publication and the contents of joint publications, the joint publications will take precedence for the activities of joint forces.

JOHN N. ABRAMS
General, U.S. Army
Commanding General
U.S. Army Training and Doctrine
   Command

B.B. KNUTSON, JR.
Lieutenant General, USMC
Commanding General
Marine Corps Combat
   Development Command

Chapter I

Authority and Functions
of
Joint Force Land Component Commander

SCOPE

I-1. This handbook is designed for planning and conducting land operations requiring the close coordination of Army forces (ARFOR) and Marine Corps forces (MARFOR) under the control of a joint force land component commander (JFLCC) within the joint operations area (JOA). Joint force land component (JFLC) command operations addressed are primarily those involving large forces to include Army divisions and Marine expeditionary forces (MEFs) and the conduct of operations outside of an amphibious objective area (AOA), if designated. This handbook is also useful for planning and conducting land operations across the range of military operations and in multinational environments.

PURPOSE

I-2. Formation, functions, and organization of the JFLC command are addressed herein. Also discussed are the operational questions of who, what, when, and how of JFLC command operations in support of a campaign by a joint force commander (JFC). Joint doctrine establishes that the JFLCC option is available to the JFC. However, the doctrine necessary for planning and executing the JFLCC concept is still evolving. This United States Army (USA)/United States Marine Corps (USMC) handbook provides information and guidance to assist readers in the forming, planning, training, and execution of the JFLCC concept.

> Functional component commands can be appropriate when forces from two or more Military Departments must operate in the same dimension or medium or there is a need to accomplish a distinct aspect of the assigned mission.
>
> Joint Pub (JP) 5-00.2

ROLE AND AUTHORITY
OF THE COMBATANT COMMANDER

I-3. Unified action demands maximum interoperability. The forces, units, and systems of all Services achieve interoperability through collective efforts to develop and use joint doctrine; joint tactics, techniques, and procedures; and through the conduct of joint training. Joint forces can be established on either a geographic or functional basis. JFCs have the authority to organize forces to best accomplish the assigned mission based on their concept of operations (CONOPS). The organization should be sufficiently flexible to meet the planned phases of the campaign or major operation and any development that necessitates a change in plan. It should also optimize the capabilities of each component while maintaining the requisite unity of effort to attain the military objectives.

FUNCTIONS OF THE COMBATANT COMMANDS

I-4. Unless otherwise directed by the President or the Secretary of Defense (SecDef), the authority, direction, and control of the commander of a combatant command (COCOM), with respect to the commands and the forces assigned to that command, are shown in Figure I-1.

- Giving authoritative direction to subordinate commands and forces necessary to carry out missions assigned to the command, including authoritative direction over all aspects of military operations, joint training, and logistics.
- Prescribing the chain of command to the commands and forces within the command.
- Organizing commands and forces within that command as necessary to carry out missions assigned to the command.
- Employing forces within that command as necessary to carry out missions assigned to the command.
- Assigning command functions to subordinate commanders.
- Coordinating and approving those aspects of administration, support (including control of resources and equipment, internal organization, and training), and discipline necessary to carry out missions assigned to the command.
- Exercising the authority with respect to selecting subordinate commanders, selecting combatant command staff, suspending subordinates, and convening courts-martial as delineated in Chapter 6, title 10, US Code.

Figure I-1. General Functions of a Combatant Commander

AUTHORITY OVER SUBORDINATE COMMANDERS

I-5.   Unless otherwise directed by the President or the SecDef—

- Commanders of commands and forces assigned to a combatant commander are under the authority, direction, and control of, and are responsible to, the combatant commander.
- The subordinate commander communicates with other elements of the Department of Defense (DOD) on matters the combatant commander is assigned authority for in accordance with procedures, if any, established by the combatant commander.
- Other elements of DOD communicate with the subordinate commander on matters the combatant commander is assigned authority for in accordance with established procedures.
- The subordinate commander advises the combatant commander, if so directed, of all communications to and from other elements of DOD on matters the combatant commander has not been assigned authority for.

A joint force commander (JFC) is a combatant commander, subunified commander, or joint task force (JTF) commander authorized to exercise combatant command (command authority) or operational control over a joint force.

FUNCTIONAL COMPONENT COMMAND AUTHORITY

I-6.   Combatant commanders and commanders of subordinate unified commands and JTFs have the authority to establish functional component commands to control military operations. Functional component commands may be established across the range of military operations to perform operational missions that may be of short or extended duration. The JFC has the authority to establish and designate a JFLCC. Functional component commands do not constitute a "joint force" with the authorities and responsibilities of a joint force as described in the United Action Armed Forces (UNAAF). Normally, the Service component commander with the majority of forces, and requisite command and control (C^2) capabilities, is designated as the functional component commander. However, the JFC considers the mission, nature and duration of the operation, force capabilities, and the C^2 capabilities in selecting a commander.

I-7. The responsibilities and authority of a functional component command are assigned by the establishing JFC. The establishment and designation of a functional component commander must not affect the command relationships between Service component commanders and the JFC.

I-8. The JFC must designate the military capability and forces that will be made available for tasking by the functional component commander and the appropriate command relationship(s) the functional component commander exercises over the forces provided.

I-9. When a functional component command will employ forces from more than one military department, the staff should be representative of the land forces that comprise the land component command.

COMMAND RELATIONSHIPS

I-10. The authority vested in a commander is commensurate with the responsibility assigned. Forces, not command relationships, are transferred between commands. When forces are transferred, the command relationship the gaining commander exercises (and the losing commander relinquishes) over those forces must be specified. The four levels of command relationships used for US military forces are—

- Combatant command.
- Operational control (OPCON).
- Tactical control (TACON).
- Support.

These command relationships are discussed in detail in Chapter II.

Chapter II

Command, Control, and Command Relationships

COMMAND RELATIONSHIPS

II-1. The four levels of command relationships used for US military forces are described below.

COMBATANT COMMAND (COMMAND AUTHORITY)

II-2. COCOM is the command authority over assigned forces vested only in the commanders of COCOMs by title 10, US Code, Section 164, or as directed by the President in the Unified Command Plan (UCP), and cannot be delegated or transferred. The combatant commander normally exercises OPCON over forces attached by the National Command Authority (NCA). Forces are attached when the transfer of forces is temporary. Establishing authorities for subordinate unified commands and JTFs will normally direct the delegation of OPCON over forces attached to those subordinate commands.

II-3. COCOM is the authority of a combatant commander to perform those functions of command over assigned forces to include—

- Organizing and employing commands and forces.
- Assigning tasks.
- Designating objectives.
- Giving authoritative direction over all aspects of military operations, joint training (or in the case of US Southern Command, training of assigned forces).
- Logistics.

II-4. COCOM should be exercised through the commanders of subordinate organizations. Normally, this authority is exercised through subordinate JFCs and Service and/or functional component commanders. COCOM provides full authority to organize and employ commands and forces as the combatant commander considers necessary to accomplish assigned missions.

OPERATIONAL CONTROL

II-5. OPCON is the command authority exercised by commanders at any echelon at or below the level of COCOM and can be delegated or transferred.

II-6. OPCON is inherent in COCOM and is the authority to perform those functions of command over subordinate forces involving—

- Organizing and employing commands and forces.
- Assigning tasks.
- Designating objectives.
- Giving authoritative direction necessary to accomplish the mission.

II-7. OPCON includes authoritative direction over all aspects of military operations and joint training necessary to accomplish missions assigned to the command. It should be exercised through the commanders of subordinate organizations; normally, this authority is exercised through subordinate JFCs and Service and/or functional component commanders. OPCON normally provides full authority to organize commands and forces and employ those forces necessary to accomplish assigned missions. It does not include authoritative direction for logistics or matters of administration, discipline, internal organization, or unit training. The combatant commander delegates these elements. OPCON does include the authority to delineate functional responsibilities and geographic JOAs of subordinate JFCs.

II-8. The superior commander gives commanders of subordinate commands and JTFs OPCON of assigned or attached forces.

TACTICAL CONTROL

II-9. TACON is the command authority over assigned or attached forces or commands, or military capability or forces made available for tasking. It is limited to the detailed and usually local direction and control of movements or maneuvers necessary to accomplish assigned missions or tasks.

II-10. TACON may be delegated to and exercised by commanders at any echelon at or below the level of COCOM. TACON is inherent in OPCON.

SUPPORT

II-11. Support is a command authority. A support relationship is established by a superior commander between subordinate commanders when one organization should aid, protect, complement, or sustain another force.

II-12. Support may be exercised by commanders at any echelon at or below the level of COCOM. This includes the NCA designating a support relationship between combatant commanders as well as within a COCOM. The designation of supporting relationships is important as it conveys priorities to commanders and staffs who are planning or executing joint operations. The support command relationship is a flexible arrangement. The establishing authority is responsible for ensuring that both the supported and supporting commanders understand the degree of authority granted the supported commander.

II-13. The supported commander should ensure that the supporting commander understands the assistance required. The supporting commander provides the assistance needed, subject to the supporting commander's existing capabilities and other assigned tasks. When the supporting commander cannot fulfill the needs of the supported commander, the establishing authority is notified by either the supported or supporting commander. The establishing authority is responsible for determining a solution.

II-14. An establishing directive is normally issued to specify the purpose of the support relationship, the effect desired, and the action to be taken.

II-15. See JP 0-2 for additional information on command relationships.

JFLC COMMAND RELATIONSHIPS

II-16. Unity of command and effort is a primary consideration when establishing a JFLC command. The JFLC command gives the JFC another option for managing the operations of land forces by reducing his span of control. JFCs may elect to centralize selected functions within the joint force, but should avoid reducing the versatility, responsiveness, and initiative of subordinate forces. The JFLCC must understand his relationship with the JFC, the other components (Service and functional), and the forces/capabilities made available. The JFLCC may provide support to other components and may similarly receive support from other Service or functional components. Likewise, as a Service component commander, the JFLCC also has responsibilities associated with Service component command for those assigned forces.

II-17. The type of command relationship given the JFLCC is based on the JFC's CONOPS and guidance. Functional component commanders typically exercise TACON over military capability or forces made available for tasking. The authority given to a functional component commander is based on mission, enemy, terrain and weather, troops and support available, and time available (METT-T). The JFC designates the military capability available to the functional component commander, and he specifies the appropriate command relationships the functional component commander exercises. Once the JFC decides to form a JFLC command, he determines both the command relationships between the JFLC command and the components (Service and functional).

II-18. The JFLCC is the focal point for planning and executing the land operations portion of the JFC's campaign plan. The JFLCC prepares a supporting joint land operations plan that provides the intent, CONOPS, and the supporting details. The JFLCC directs current land operations while continuing to plan and prepare for future land operations.

COMMAND RELATIONSHIPS WITH THE JFC

II-19. The JFLCC reports directly to the JFC and advises the JFC on the proper employment of land forces. The JFC has the full authority to assign missions, redirect efforts, and direct coordination among subordinate commanders. JFCs should allow Service tactical and operational assets and groupings to function as they are designed. The intent is to meet the needs of the JFC while maintaining the tactical and operational integrity of the Service organizations.

COMMAND RELATIONSHIPS WITH FUNCTIONAL COMPONENTS

II-20. The JFC may also establish supporting and supported relationships between components. The JFC determines not only how to organize the joint force into components, but also how each component relates to the others. Support relationships afford an effective means to weight (and ensure unity of effort for) the main effort of various operations, each component typically receiving and providing support at the same time.

II-21. As with all other authority within a joint force, support authority is directed by the JFC. There are four support relationships directed by the JFC: general support, mutual support, close support, and direct support.

- General Support. Support given to the supported force as a whole and not to any particular subdivision thereof.
- Mutual Support. Support units render each other against an adversary. This is based on, because of their assigned tasks, their position relative to each other and to the adversary, and their inherent capabilities.
- Close Support. Action of the supporting force against targets or objectives which are sufficiently close to the supported force. This requires detailed integration or coordination of the supporting action with the fire, movement, or other actions of the supported force.
- Direct Support. A mission requiring a force to support another specific unit. This authorizes the supporting unit to answer directly to the supported force's request for assistance.

II-22. Regardless of the organizational and command arrangements within joint commands, Service component commanders are responsible for certain Service-specific functions and other matters affecting their forces, including internal administration, training, logistics, and Service intelligence operations.

Combatant commanders, commanders of subordinate unified commands, and joint task forces (JTFs) have the authority to establish functional component commands to control military operations.

JP 0-2

FUNCTIONAL COMPONENT SUPPORT RELATIONSHIPS

II-23. The JFLC command can be in either a supporting or supported relationship or both. The JFC's needs for unity of command and unity of effort dictate these relationships. Support relationships will be established by the JFC in appropriate campaign plans and orders. Similar relationships can be established among all functional and Service component commanders, such as the coordination of deep operations involving the JFLC command and the joint force air component commander (JFACC). Close coordination is necessary when the JFLCC provides joint suppression of enemy air defenses in support of JFACC operations. Examples are attack helicopters or multiple-launched rocket systems in Operation DESERT STORM as well as seizing and holding ports and airbases for friendly air and sea forces (such as in Operation JUST CAUSE). The JFLCC can also expect support to include airlift, close air support (CAS), and interdiction strikes from the JFACC.

II-24. The JFC may task the JFLCC to conduct operations outside of the land AO. Land-based elements may conduct air and missile defense operations to protect the force and critical assets from air and missile attack and surveillance. These may include operational maneuver and/or operational fires against enemy ports and airbases outside of the land area of operations (AO). Similarly, the JFLCC can request from the JFC air support from other components to attack or isolate enemy land forces in the land AO. Figure II-1 illustrates a simultaneous support relationship scenario between the JFLCC and JFACC.

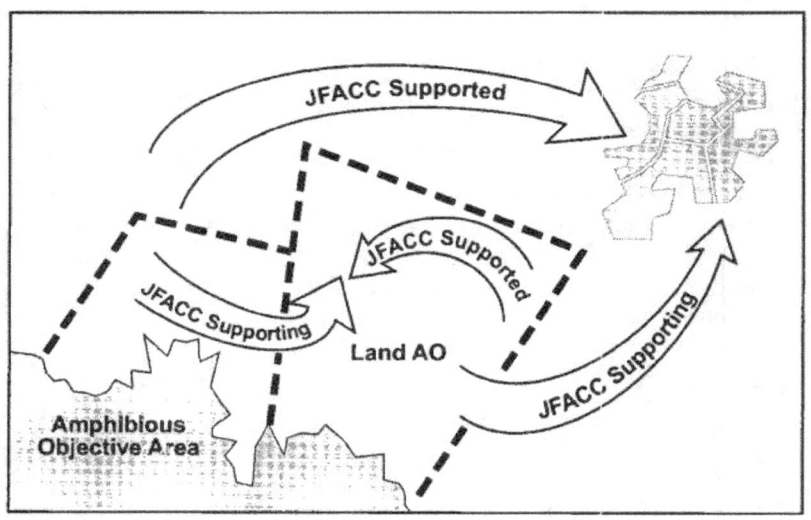

Figure II-1. JFLCC and JFACC Support Relationships

COMMAND RELATIONSHIPS
WITH SERVICE COMPONENTS

II-25. The JFLC command functional component responsibility is normally assigned to a commander already serving as a Service component (e.g.,

ARFOR, MARFOR) to a JTF or subordinate unified command. Additionally, the JFC may use one of his Service components (e.g., Army Service component or Marine Service component) as the JFLCC reporting to him directly. The JFLCC retains Service component responsibility for assigned or attached forces but does not assume Service component responsibility for forces made available by other Service components. TACON is the normal relationship with these Service forces. In those cases in which the JFLC command is not formed from a Service component headquarters, the JFLCC has no Service component responsibilities. (See Figure II-2.)

II-26. Once the JFLC command is established, the operational requirements of the JFLCC subordinate commands are prioritized and presented to the joint force headquarters by the JFLCC. However, Service component commanders remain responsible for their military department Title 10 responsibilities, such as logistics and personnel support. See Appendix C for details.

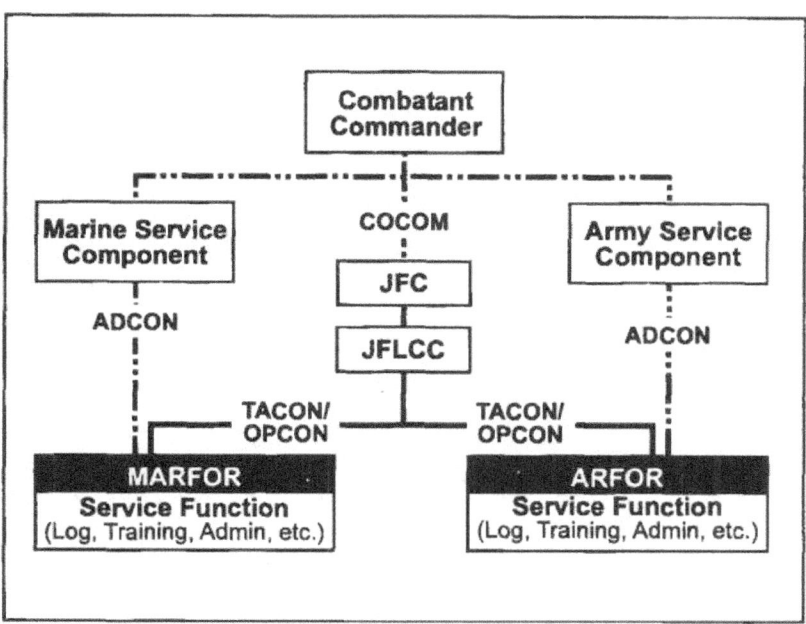

Figure II-2. Service Functions

LIAISON

II-27. Command relationships and mission accomplishment determine LNO requirements.

> Liaison officers (LNOs) facilitate the communication maintained between elements of a JTF to ensure mutual understanding and unity of purpose and action....Typically, LNOs are exchanged between higher, lower, and adjacent units....Additionally, LNOs may be provided from government agencies, nongovernmental organizations (NGOs), international organizations, or private voluntary organizations (PVOs).
>
> ALSA JTF Liaison Handbook

ORGANIZATION

II-28. The JFLC command establishes liaison with other components to facilitate supporting and supported command relationships and to coordinate the planning and execution of land operations. The JFLC command considers existing liaison requirements from ARFOR and MARFOR when establishing liaison requirements with the JFACC for joint fire support. The JFLC command must be prepared to receive and integrate other component liaison teams, such as Joint Force Maritime Component Command (JFMCC) and Joint Force Special Operations Component Command (JFSOCC).

II-29. The JFC determines whether LNOs will be provided by both Service components (ARFOR and MARFOR) and JFLC command headquarters or to simply have the JFLC command perform the liaison role for the total land force.

II-30. In those cases where the JFLCC is representing the total land force, the LNO team should include both Army and Marine officers. The JFLCC should also designate a senior LNO from the team as the official spokesperson for the JFLCC.

II-31. The JFLCC LNO team represents the JFLCC as a single force and addresses particular issues unique to their individual Service.

II-32. LNO teams may represent the JFLCC at various meetings of joint force and component boards, centers, and cells including joint planning group (JPG), information operations (IO) cell, joint targeting coordination board (JTCB), and civil-military operations center (CMOC).

FUNCTIONS

> LNOs, whether individually or in teams, perform several critical functions that are consistent across the full range of military operations. The extent that these functions are performed is dependent on the mission and the charter established by the sending organization commander they represent. A successful LNO performs four basic functions: monitor, coordinate, advise, and assist.
>
> ALSA JTF Liaison Handbook

II-33. The LNO monitors the development of plans and current operations of the JFLCC and the headquarters he is tasked to liaison with. He must know the current situation and planned operations, understand pertinent staff issues, and the JFC's and JFLCC's mission, intent, and concept for the operation.

II-34. The LNO facilitates the synchronization and integration of current operations and future plans between the JFLCC and the JFC or components. This is accomplished through coordination with other LNOs, the JFC staff, and the JFLCC staff. The LNO must anticipate JTF and JFLCC information requirements. Coordination by the LNO complements rather than competes with normal staff coordination.

II-35. The LNO is a valuable subject matter expert on capabilities and limitations of the land component for the JFC and component commanders. As such, the LNO advises the JFC commander and staff on the optimum employment of the JFLC command's capabilities. Additionally, the LNO advises the JFLCC and staff on any JFC issues and activities of other components. LNOs must exercise caution to ensure that they do not obligate the JFLCC beyond the authority provided.

II-36. The LNOs assist on two levels. First, they act as the conduit between the JFLCC and the JFC. Second, by integrating themselves into the joint force staff as a participant in the daily battle rhythm (the daily briefings, meetings, planning sessions, etc.), the LNOs can answer questions from various groups (JTCB, JPG, command group, etc.) to ensure that those groups make informed decisions.

LNO REQUIREMENTS

II-37. The gaining unit should first identify and define requirements for LNOs/teams. There may be specific requirements for an LNO or liaison team that include rank, Service, weapon system specialty, and experience. There may be unique administrative requirements to include medical, training, passport/visa, country clearances, interpreter skills, and uniform/equipment. The gaining unit should plan to integrate the LNOs/teams and provide support to include billeting/messing, workspace, administrative/service, publication/documents, and equipment for follow-on movements/deployments.

LNO RESPONSIBILITIES

II-38. LNO/LNO team responsibilities include—

- Understanding the mission, the commander's expectations, specific responsibilities to the sending and gaining organizations, and the command relationship that will exist between the sending and gaining organizations, as well as other major commands participating in the operation.
- Being familiar with potential issues of the JFLCC, including specific issues and information requirements from each staff section.
- Knowing the current situation of the JFLCC to include the commander's intent, commander's critical information requirements (CCIR), time-phased force and deployment data (TPFDD) issues, and CONOPS.
- Contacting the headquarters requiring liaison prior to departure to determine any special requirements to include equipment, operations security (OPSEC) applicable to the mission, arrangements for communications, etc., the LNO must accomplish.

- Informing the commander and staff of the JFLCC's intent and guidance concerning land operations and all activities within the JFLCC's AO.
- Updating the commander and staff on the JFLCC's priority, timing, and effects for supported actions.
- Monitoring and interpreting the land battle situation for the commander and his staff.
- Keeping informed of the operational status of units.

PLANNING

II-39. The joint operation planning at the JFLC command headquarters is predominately at the operational level of war. Land force planning links the tactical employment of land forces to campaign and strategic objectives. The focus at the command level is on operational art—the use of military forces to achieve strategic objectives through the design, organization, and execution of strategies, campaigns, major operations, and battles.

II-40. Operational art determines when, where, and for what purpose major forces are employed and should influence the enemy disposition before combat. It governs the deployment of those forces, their commitment to or withdrawal from battle, and the arrangement of battles and major operations to achieve operational and strategic objectives.

II-41. JFLCC operational planning addresses some activities required for conducting joint/multinational land operations. These activities include—

- Employment planning which describes how to apply force/forces to attain specified military objectives.
- Sustainment planning which is directed toward providing and maintaining levels of personnel, materiel, and consumables required to sustain the levels of combat activity for the estimated duration and at the desired level of intensity.

PROCESS

II-42. The JFLCC conducts planning using the planning processes of the command that forms the core of the headquarters. While almost all headquarters use the Joint Operation Planning and Execution System (JOPES) planning cycle described in joint planning publications, the specific steps in the process may have different names and somewhat different activities. JFLC command staff members, provided by Services other than the core of the headquarters and integrated into the core staff, must quickly adapt to the planning processes and battle rhythm of the staff they are joining.

II-43. The primary difference between planning for single-Service forces and JFLC command forces is the addition of unique capabilities and limitations of each force. This requires an understanding of these capabilities and limitations across all staff functions, but it is particularly important in the JPG. JPGs must have knowledgeable members from each Service in all functional areas. With these key personnel and appropriate LNOs from the major subordinate commands in place, the planning process provides sufficient consideration of the capabilities of each Service.

II-44. The force deployment planning conducted by the deployment cell in J-5 must be in concert with the JPG's operational planning. The deployment planners require visibility on the capabilities and sequencing priorities associated with a course of action (COA) or CONOPS to ensure they are transportable and the deployment requirements are relayed to the JFLC command forces and JFC. The JFLC command planning staff must remember that the timing and sequencing priority may be effected by the JFC's overall concept of deployment.

PRODUCTS

II-45. JFLCC operation plans (OPLANs), concept plans (CONPLANs), and/or operations orders (OPORDs) convey how the land force helps achieve the JFC's mission. The JFLCC plan describes the relationship or arrangement of major land operations that accomplish the JFC's strategic and operational objectives. The plan incorporates appropriate elements of operational art and fundamentals of joint/multinational warfare and military operations other than war (MOOTW).

II-46. The OPORD describes the synchronization of specific tasks that result in a synergistic employment of joint/multinational land force capabilities for a major operation. The format for the OPORD generally follows that found in JP 5-00.2

II-47. OPLANs, CONPLANs, and OPORDs are distributed internally to the land force and externally to the JFC and Service and functional component commands for information. If OPLANS, CONPLANS, or OPORDs describe a branch or sequel to the current plan, they are distributed externally to the JFC for approval and to the Service and functional component commands and land force subordinate commands for information. Once approved, the JFC provides additional instructions to the land force.

II-48. Planning products are distributed simultaneously to all JFLC commands. JFLCC subordinate commands can adequately evaluate the impact of future operations and plans from an operational aspect; however, the Service component command headquarters must be concurrently involved to assist in assessing ability of subordinate units to support the JFLCC.

II-49. Upon completion of the planning products and orders, the JPG organizes to conduct execution phase planning. This represents an organizational strategy describing the transfer of responsibilities, products, and time-flow of planning documents through the planning staff. This depicts one means of forwarding planning products from the planners to those responsible for execution. Key to the success of the plans handoff is the requirement that the organization responsible for execution has enough background, rationale, and understanding of the plan (branch or sequel) to effectively execute it. Experience has shown that the current operations cell is often too immersed in ongoing operations to plan outside the current 24-hour period.

COMMUNICATIONS

II-50. The combatant commander. through the subordinate JFC and Service component commands, ensures effective and efficient command, control, communications, and computer (C^4) system services consistent with the overall joint campaign plan. As driven by the mission, the foundation of the C^4 system is laid by the C^2 organization of forces assigned to the JFC. All C^4 intelligence systems and upgrades will comply with the DOD Joint Technical Architecture.

II-51. The JFLCC provides, by exception only, standardized direction and guidance on joint C^4 matters to the command as they affect the operational mission. The JFLCC may delegate responsibility for the accomplishment of joint C^4 tasks under the OPCON of the JFLCC.

CONCEPT

II-52. The JFC develops the overarching campaign plan in concert with the combatant commander's guidance and with input from subordinate Service component and functional component commands. Based on guidance from the

JFC, the JFLCC develops the land operations portion of the campaign plan. The plan is then provided to the JFC for developing and coordinating employment of forces and support of the overall campaign plan. The individual Service component commands, however, have the overall responsibility for providing C^4 to their own forces unless otherwise directed. (See Figure II-3.)

II-53. In carrying out the duties of the JFLCC, communications connectivity utilizes the existing joint theater communications system (TCS) which is directed, established, and managed by the JFC. This provides robust theaterwide voice, data, and message connectivity between all components and elements. In addition, TCS addresses unique communications connectivity requirements that provide for the appropriate interface between ARFOR and MARFOR forces and C^2 that permits timely execution of assigned missions.

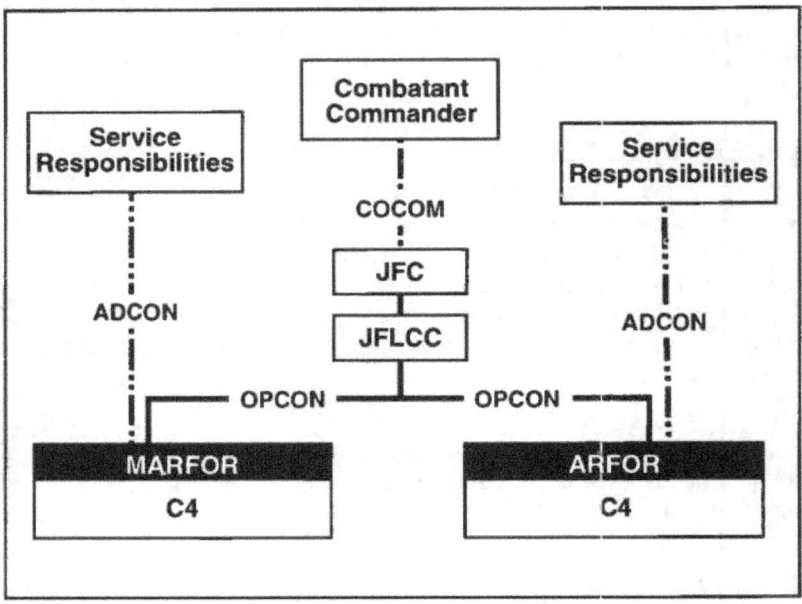

Figure II-3. Communications

II-54. Tactical communications in the AO are phased in and established as specified in the OPLAN and/or OPORD being supported/executed.

II-55. Technical guidance and procedures contained in CJCS instructions and manuals; allied communications publications; Joint Army, Navy, Air Force publications; and DOD directives will apply. In the case where individual Service doctrine conflicts with joint doctrine, joint procedures are followed.

COMMAND RELATIONSHIPS

II-56. The JFLCC exercises OPCON of all forces assigned for the accomplishment of the mission on an exception basis. Communication hardware is a Service component responsibility and only those communication issues affecting the conduct of the operational mission are of concern to the JFLCC J-6.

ROLE OF THE JFLCC J-6

II-57. The JFLCC J-6 provides critical functional expertise to the JFLCC in the C^4 areas. These primary staff officers focus on key C^4 issues that may have an adverse affect on the land portion of the joint campaign. Generally, they manage by exception only. Routine C^4 management is the responsibility of the JFC and the subordinate Service component commands. Appendix G has more information regarding the organization and responsibilities of the J-6 staff.

Chapter III

Responsibilities, Roles, and Functions

JFLCC RESPONSIBILITIES AND ROLES

III-1. The JFLCC's overall responsibilities and roles are to organize, plan, and direct execution of land operations based upon the JFC's concept of operations and designation of command relationships. The responsibilities of the JFLCC include, but are not limited to:

- Advising the JFC on the proper employment of all assigned and attached forces.

- Developing a land OPLAN/OPORD that supports the operational objectives of the JFC and optimizes the operations of task-organized land forces. The JFLCC issues planning guidance to all subordinate and supporting elements and analyzes proposed COAs. The intent is to concentrate the effects of combat power at critical times and places to accomplish operational or strategic goals.

- Directing the execution of the land OPLAN/OPORD as specified by the JFC, which includes making timely adjustments to the tasking of assigned/attached forces. The JFLCC coordinates changes with effected component commanders as appropriate.

- Coordinating the planning and execution of land operations with the other component, JTF commanders, and other supporting agencies.

- Evaluating the results of land operations to include the effectiveness of interdiction operations and forwarding these results to the JFC to support the combat assessment (CA) effort.

- Synchronizing and integrating movement and maneuver, firepower, CAS, and interdiction in support of the land operations. As a member of the JTCB, the JFLCC designates the target priorities, effects, and timing within his AO.

- Supporting the JFACC for counterair operations, strategic attack, theater airborne reconnaissance and surveillance, and theater- and/or JOA-wide interdiction effort. Once the JFC designates a land AO, the land force commander is supported by other components within his AO.

- Providing the deputy area air defense commander (DAADC) for land-based air and missile defense or joint theater missile defense (JTMD) as determined by the JFC.

- Supporting the JFC IO by developing the IO requirements that support land-control operations and synchronizing the land force IO assets when directed.

- Establishing combat identification standing operating procedures and other directives based on JFC guidance.

JFLCC FUNCTIONS

III-2. The JFLCC and his staff perform, or contribute to, a number of core functions that are critical for successfully conducting land operations. These functions apply in varying degrees across the range of military operations including those involving multinational forces. These functions are—

- Movement and maneuver.
- Intelligence, surveillance, reconnaissance (ISR).
- Firepower.
- Logistics and personnel support.
- C^2.
- Force protection.

These functions are performed through the execution of operational tasks that form a comprehensive rationalization of how the JFLCC conducts operations at the operational level. The six operational functions are listed below in Figure III-1. See CJCS Memorandum 3500.04B for details.

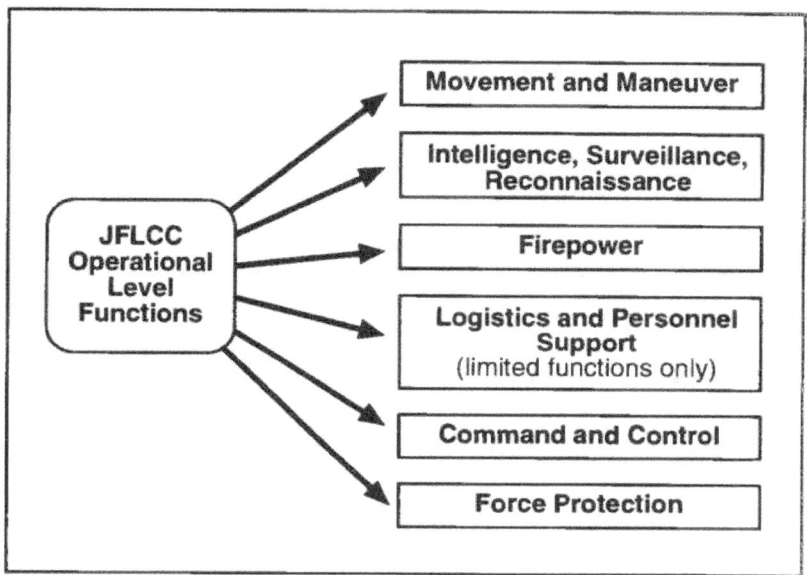

Figure III-1. JFLCC Operational Functions

MOVEMENT AND MANEUVER

III-3. The JFLCC is responsible for land component operational movement and maneuver necessary to contribute to the success of the JFC's campaign. He directs the land force in performance of operational tasks and influences lateral and higher headquarters in terms of either supporting the land force or assigning further operational tasks. The JFLCC makes recommendations to the JFC on the employment and support of land forces. This includes the following:

- Force structure.
- Integration and employment of multinational land forces.
- Land force scheme of maneuver and fire support.
- Priorities of effort for land forces.
- Designating the fire support coordination measures (FSCMs) and JFLCC boundaries with his AO.
- Intelligence collection priorities.
- Joint fire support for the land forces.

- Joint fires to support other components.
- Space support to the land force.
- Input on the airspace control measures in the airspace within the JFLCC AO boundaries

INTELLIGENCE, SURVEILLANCE, RECONNAISSANCE

III-4. The JFLCC states operational requirements and provides continuous feedback to ensure optimum intelligence support to operations. This interface is essential to the following purposes of intelligence:

- To support the commander.
- To identify, define, and nominate objectives.
- To support operational planning and execution.
- To avoid surprise.
- To assist friendly deception efforts.
- To evaluate the effects of operations.

At the operational level, all major tactical combat formations share in access to the joint intelligence architecture. The JFLCC may prioritize land force subordinate requests for information (RFI) including the identification and location of enemy center(s) of gravity (COGs) that could be successfully attacked by land forces. (See Appendix A.)

FIREPOWER

III-5. The JFLCC is responsible for the planning and employment of operational firepower both in terms of developing an integrated multidimensional/multimedium attack on the adversary's COG and in terms of shaping the land forces' future battlefield. The JFLCC should provide guidance for the employment of operational firepower, including lethal and nonlethal means, to shape the battlespace and influence conditions for future operations. (See Appendix D.)

LOGISTICS AND PERSONNEL SUPPORT

III-6. Each Service is responsible for the logistics support of its own forces, except when logistics support is otherwise provided for by agreement with national agencies, multinational partners, or by assignments to common, joint, or cross servicing. The supported COCOM may determine that common servicing would be beneficial within the theater or designated area. The JFLCC would make recommendations concerning the distribution of materiel and services commensurate with priorities developed for land force operations. (See Appendix C.)

COMMAND AND CONTROL

III-7. The JFLCC has significant responsibility for operational C^2 in that he becomes the single focal point for integrated and synchronized land force operations for the JFC. Upon approval of the land force plan, the JFLCC exercises specified authority and direction over the land forces in the accomplishment of the land force mission. JFLCC responsibility is to C^2 land operations to ensure they accomplish campaign and major operations objectives. A JFLCC staff is established either through liaison, augmentation, or through the development of a dedicated staff with representation that is ideally proportional to the mix of forces. The JFLCC must maintain liaison and representation on JTF boards, groups, and cells. These include IO cell, JTCB, JPG, CMOC, among others. Representation is essential to ensuring that land force operations are coordinated and achieve unity of effort for the JFC. Additionally, JFLCC assists the JFC in long-range or future planning, preparation of campaign and joint operation plans, and associated estimates of the situation. JFLCC tasks include the following:

- Preparing and coordinating required land component OPLANs or OPORDs in support of assigned JFC missions.
- Coordinating land component planning efforts with higher, lower, adjacent, and multinational headquarters as required.
- Developing land component COAs within the framework of the JFC-assigned objective or mission, forces available, and the commander's intent. Determining land component forces required and available and coordinating force projection planning in support of the selected COAs.

III-8. The JFLCC is responsible for developing and integrating the land component C^4 architecture and plans that support the JFC's operational requirements. Additionally, JFLCC establishes the policy and guidance for land component implementation and integration of interoperable C^4 systems to exercise command in the execution of the land component mission. The JFLCC provides standardized direction and guidance on C^4 matters to the joint command and any other communications supporting elements. The

JFLCC may delegate responsibility for the accomplishment of joint C^4 tasks that are under his OPCON. In situations where the establishment of a JFLCC staff is on short notice, the participating Services will be challenged to provide communications resources necessary for standing up the C^4 architecture. The Service component designated as the command will primarily be responsible for C^4 resources.

FORCE PROTECTION

III-9. The JFLCC significantly influences the JFC force protection plans and priorities—particularly land component operations. The JFLCC is responsible to the JFC for all land force protection operations. Force protection includes the following elements:

- Defensive counterair (DCA) (air defense and JTMD).
- Nuclear, biological, chemical (NBC) defense.
- Combating terrorism to include antiterrorism (AT) programs.
- Defensive IO.
- Security for operational forces and means.
- Physical security.
- OPSEC.

A listing and description of these operational functions are at Appendix E.

MULTINATIONAL CONSIDERATIONS

III-10. Effectively planned and executed multinational operations should, in addition to achieving common objectives, facilitate unity of effort without diminishing freedom of action and preserve unit integrity and uninterrupted support. Each multinational operation is unique, and key considerations involved in planning and conducting multinational operations vary with the international situation and perspectives, motives, and values of the organization's members.

III-11. The following key considerations for multinational operations are addressed in JP 3-16 and Appendix G:

- Mission analysis and assignment of tasks.
- Political and military considerations.
- Intelligence and information.
- Logistics and host-nation support.

- Language, culture, and sovereignty.
- Health service support.
- Termination and transition.
- Communications.
- Force protection.
- International law.
- Law of armed conflict.
- Rules of engagement (ROE).
- Doctrine, training, and resources.
- Media.
- Religious ministry support.
- Meteorology and oceanography.
- Environmental considerations.

Chapter IV

Considerations for Forming a JFLC Command

ESTABLISHING AUTHORITY

IV-1. A JFC has the authority to organize forces to best accomplish the assigned mission based on the CONOPS. The JFC establishes subordinate commands, assigns responsibilities, establishes or delegates appropriate command and support relationships, and establishes coordinating instructions for the component commanders. Sound organization provides for unity of effort, centralized planning, and decentralized execution. Unity of effort is necessary for effectiveness and efficiency. Centralized planning is essential for controlling and coordinating the efforts of the forces. When organizing joint forces with multinational forces, simplicity and clarity are critical.

IV-2. JP 3-0 states that "functional commands are established to provide centralized direction and control of certain functions and types of operations". The JFC can establish functional component commands and define the authority and responsibilities of the functional component commanders based upon the CONOPS and may alter this authority during the course of an operation. Normally, this authority does not include forming subordinate functional commands or reorganizing forces that have been assigned or made available.

IV-3. The designation of a JFLCC may occur when major land forces of more than one Service component participate in a land operation, and the JFC ascertains that doing this will achieve unity of command and effort among land forces.

DEFINING THE AREA OF OPERATIONS

IV-4. An AO is an operational area defined for the JFLCC by the JFC. The AO is most likely outside an AOA. See JPs 3-0 and 3-02 for additional guidance on AOAs.

IV-5. AOs do not typically encompass the entire JOA. However, the AO should be large enough for the JFLCC to accomplish his mission and protect the force. He establishes an operational framework for the AO that assigns battlespace responsibilities to subordinate land commanders. Battlespace is the environment, factors, and conditions that must be understood to successfully apply combat power, protect the force, or complete the mission. Within the AO, battlespace includes—

- Land.
- Air.
- Sea.
- Space.
- Adversary.
- Friendly forces.
- Facilities.
- Weather.
- Terrain.
- Areas of interest (AOI).
- Portion of the information environment that affects the operation.
- Intermediate support bases (ISBs) or other force projection bases.
- Unit home stations.

IV-6. This battlespace geometry should maximize the operational capabilities of all subordinate elements. Figure IV-1 depicts this framework. When considering geometry, the MARFOR has a requirement for more battlespace than would be expected for the land force involved. This is due to the fixed-wing aviation assets that are organic to the Marine Air Ground Task Force (MAGTF).

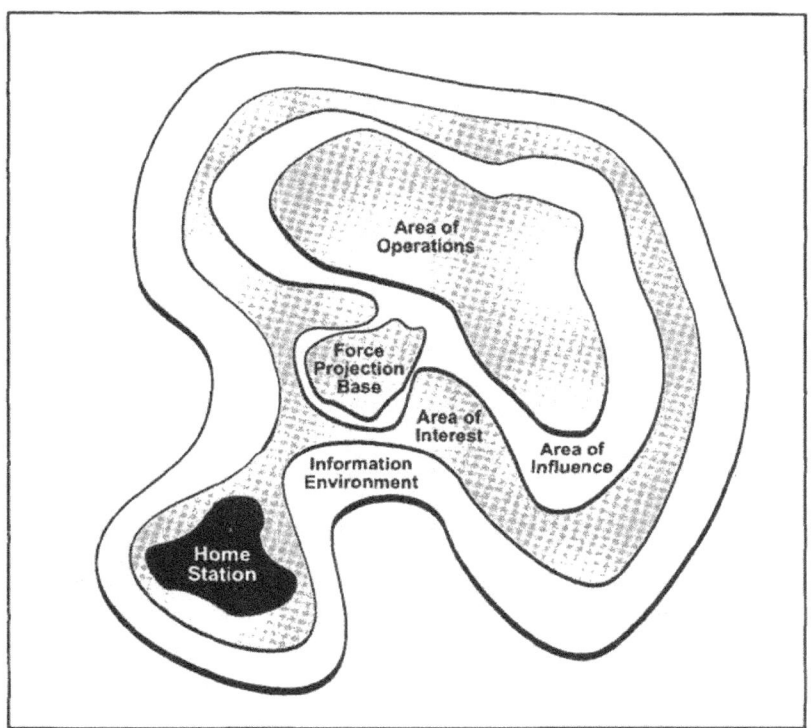

Figure IV-1. Battlespace Geometry

IV-7. The JFLCC may subdivide some or all of the assigned AOs by assigning subordinate unit AOs. These subordinate unit AOs may be contiguous or noncontiguous. When JFLC command forces are contiguous, a shared boundary separates the tactical units. In a noncontiguous environment, the tactical units of the land force do not share a common boundary. Operation JUST CAUSE is an excellent example of an operation with noncontiguous AO. The intervening area between forces remains the responsibility of the JFLCC. Figure IV-2 illustrates contiguous and noncontiguous AOs.

Contiguous Areas of Operations	Noncontiguous Areas of Operations
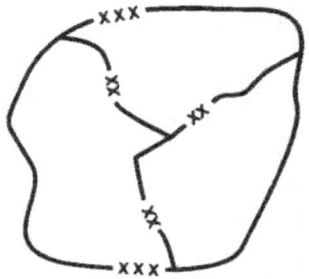	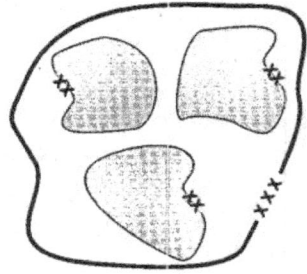
Adjacent, subordinate unit AOs share boundaries. In this case, the higher headquarters has assigned all of its AO to subordinate units.	Subordinate units receive AOs that do not share boundaries. The higher headquarters retains responsibility for the unassigned portion of its AO.

Figure IV-2. Contiguous and Noncontiguous AOs

ORGANIZING

IV-8. Several options are available for organizing a joint land force. The manner in which JFCs organize their forces directly affects the responsiveness and versatility of joint force operations. As such, joint force organizational design is heavily influenced by METT-T factors. JFCs organize all forces assigned to accomplish the mission based on the JFC's vision and CONOPS. As previously mentioned unity of effort, centralized planning, and decentralized execution are key considerations. JFCs may elect to centralize selected functions within the joint force but should strive to avoid reducing the versatility, responsiveness, and initiative of subordinate forces. JFCs can conduct operations through sub-unified commands, JTFs, Service components, functional components, or a combination of Service and functional components.

IV-9. There are four primary options available to the JFC for organizing land forces from two or more components. The four options are—

- Functional JTF.
- One Service component TACON to another.
- Maintain Service componency.
- Formation of a JFLC command.

IV-10. Each option has advantages and disadvantages which the JFC and staff must consider prior to a decision to organize under a particular option. The following advantages and disadvantages are not all-inclusive but highlight some of the more important issues.

FUNCTIONAL JTF

IV-11. The advantages are—

- Unity of command and effort.
- Joint staff.
- Authority of a JFC including the authority to organize subordinate functional components.

IV-12. The disadvantages are—

- Separate JTF commander/staff required.
- Lead time required to establish headquarters before execution.

ONE SERVICE COMPONENT TACON TO ANOTHER

IV-13. The advantages are—

- Simplified C^2.
- Efficient staff action

IV-14. The disadvantages are—

- Staff not integrated (LNO only).
- Potential for ineffective use of assigned forces.

MAINTAIN SERVICE COMPONENT ORGANIZATION

IV-15. The advantages are—

- Requires no change in structure.
- JFC directly integrates land control operations with other operations.

IV-16. The disadvantages are—

- JFC must focus on the land battle.
- Potential for JFC to lose focus on the operational-to-strategic interface.
- No single focus for land forces.
- No effective relationship between land forces and joint force component.

JFLC COMMAND STRUCTURE

IV-17. The advantages are—

- Unity of effort.
- Integrated staff.
- Single voice for land forces (consolidated picture of land force capabilities to the JFC, staff, and boards).
- Single battle concept and focus of effort for land operations (an aspect of the plan rather than a function of coordination either horizontally or vertically).
- Synchronized/integrated land force planning and execution (prioritization therefore deconfliction of competing land force requirements).

IV-18. The disadvantages are—

- JFLCC generally retains Service component responsibilities to the JFC (requires split focus of the staff).
- Challenge of integrating staffs.
- Lead time required to establish headquarters before execution.
- Sourcing the staffs.

EMPLOYING

IV-19. Considerations for employing a JFLCC are summarized as follows:

- Mission. The mission requires the unique capabilities and functions of more than one Service be directed toward closely related land objectives where unity of effort is a primary concern. Land forces are competing for limited joint force assets. The JFLCC contributes to the prioritization and control of joint force assets, as the situation requires.

- Scope. When the scope of land operations is large, the JFC needs to divide attention between major operations or phases of operations that are functionally dominated and synchronize those operations. It may be useful, therefore, to establish functionally oriented commanders responsible for the major operations.

  - Scope of forces. A JFLCC may be established anytime that the land forces of two Services are employed. A JFLCC is normally established for major theater operations where multiple corps/MEFs are employed. In some situations involving smaller forces that require Army/Marine Corps integration, the interrelationship is covered by the information provided in ALSA publication *Army and Marine Corps Integration in Joint Operations (AMCI)*, FM 90-31, MCRP 3-3.8, May 1996.

  - Scope of the AOs. Geographically concentrated land control operations may require direction by a JFLCC. Dispersed objectives, different lines of operation, and support might better be addressed by other organizational options.

- Level of operations. When the scope of the operation requires an operational level command to directly link land control operations to campaign or strategic objectives, a JFLCC can provide the linkage.

- Planning. The formation of a JFLCC integrates planning, beneath the level of the JFC, for land control operations. While this integrated planning is focused on employment, the JFLCC may also integrate planning of deployment, transition, and redeployment.

- Duration. Duration of operations must be long enough to warrant the establishment of a single land force commander. The duration of operations must be worth the costs in terms of lead time, personnel and staff training, C^4 architecture, and impact on flexibility.

- Experience. Formation of a JFLCC may enhance the detailed planning, coordination, and execution of operations required by the joint force headquarters.

- Span of control. The multiple complex tasks confronting the JFC may exceed the JFC's span of control. Having a JFLCC allows resolution of joint issues at the functional component level. The JFC has other responsibilities in the joint operating area that may require greater focus.

- Multinational operations. In multinational operations, land forces may be provided by a variety of national components. When proper authority grants organizing subordinate multinational units, the formation of a multinational force land component commander is subject to the same considerations as in US Joint Force operations.

TIMING

IV-20. The timing of the decision to designate a JFLCC is determined by the JFC. A JFC establishes a JTF to provide the requisite C^2 of the operation, or he may elect to have the components report directly to the combatant commander. Components, such as JFLCC, should be designated as early as possible. The decision to establish and designate a JFLCC ideally is during concept development of the campaign plan.

IV-21. Subordinate commanders should report to the JFLCC for planning during concept development. Subordinate commanders report to the JFLCC in sufficient time for employment operations and when the C^2 structure is established.

FORMING THE STAFF

IV-22. Once the JFC has decided to designate a JFLCC, the JFLC command headquarters is organized according to the mission and forces assigned. Normally, it is built around an existing Army or Marine headquarters staff. The core staff needs to be augmented with Army and Marine staff as soon as practical.

IV-23. Appendix F depicts a notional JFLC command staff organization. However, the organization of the Service component core staff that forms the nucleus of the command headquarters may take precedence. The standard operating procedures (SOP) for the predominant Service normally forms the baseline for the JFLC command SOP. However, supplemental SOPs are required to conduct operations with Service-unique capabilities. The training and exercising of the JFLCC staff before the conduct of operations is critical to the overall success of the mission.

FORMING THE COMMAND ELEMENT

IV-24. There are two basic options for forming the JFLC command headquarters under the joint force or JTF.

IV-25. Option A is an example of how to form the JFLC command headquarters as a separate entity from either component. This option provides the JFLCC the requisite C^2 resources to focus on the land operations without the direct responsibilities associated with logistical and administrative support. The JFLC command has a separate ARFOR and MARFOR commander and headquarters responsible for the C^2 of their respective services. Within the JFLC command headquarters, the billets of deputy commander/chief of staff and key members of the staff (J-1 through J-6) should be fully integrated with Army and USMC representation (See Figure IV-3).

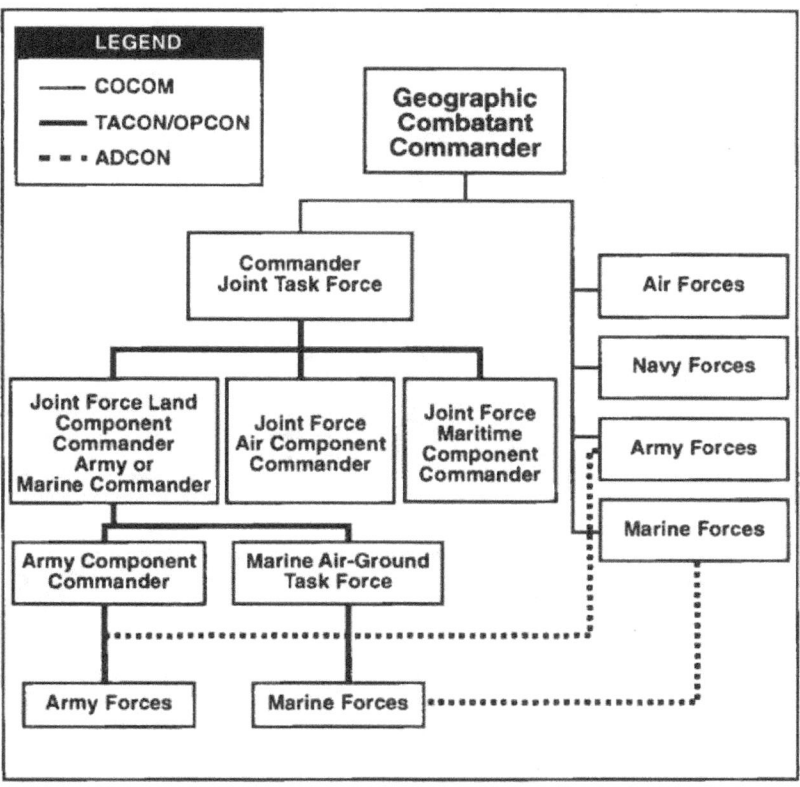

Figure IV-3. Separate JFLC Command Headquarters (Option A)

IV-26. Option B is an example of how to form the JFLC command by designating either of the JFC's Service component commanders (ARFOR or MARFOR) as the JFLCC. The JFLC command headquarters must continue to perform the Service component functions. This option also requires the other Service to be fully integrated across all staff sections. The Service designated as the JFLCC provides the core elements of the staff to assist in planning, coordinating, and executing JFLC command operations. While this option requires fewer personnel, it has the potential to overtask the JFLC command staff during the performance of their dual roles. It may be advantageous for the Service component commander to delegate as many of the Service component related duties as practical to a subordinate Service force headquarters. (See Figures IV-4 and IV-5.)

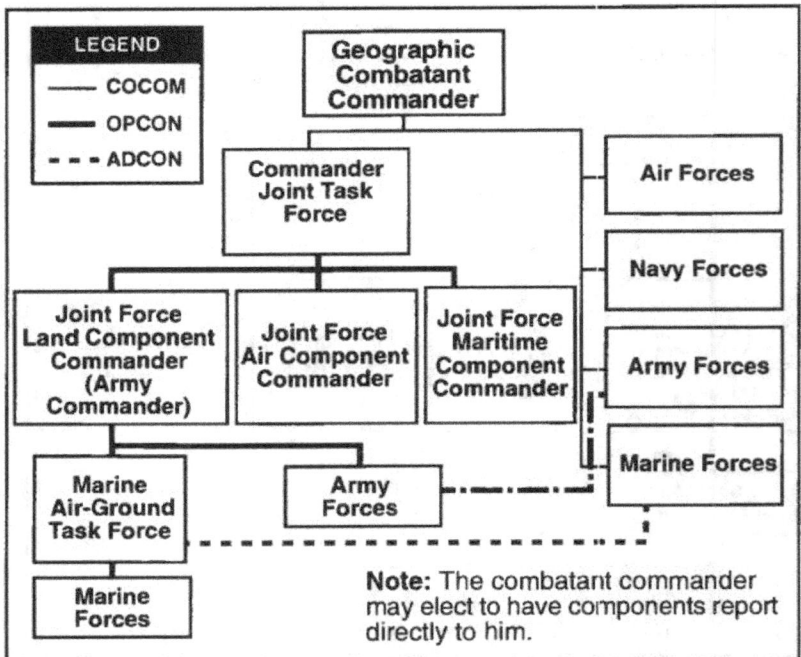

Figure IV-4. Army Commander Designated as JFLCC (Option B)

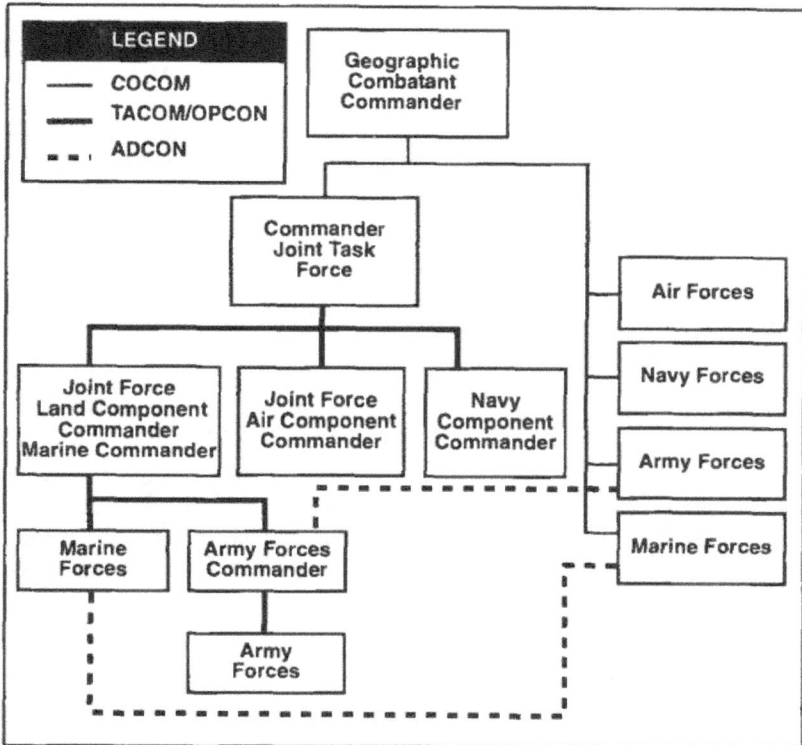

Figure IV-5. Marine Commander Designated as JFLCC (Option B)

SOURCING THE FORCES

IV-27. The forces assigned to the JFLCC are identified during the deliberate planning process. Forces are apportioned to the combatant commander in the *Forces for Unified Commands* memorandum and the UCP, and, for deliberate planning purposes, are designated in the Joint Strategic Capabilities Plan. In addition, forces are allocated to combatant commanders in response to crises.

IV-28. As the JFC develops his CONOPS, the Service and functional components conduct parallel planning. During this process, the JFC tasks the functional and Service components to provide estimates of forces required. Since the JFLCC employs Army, Marine, and, possibly, multinational land forces, he should provide his force estimate in terms of capabilities (i.e., maneuver force equivalents) required rather than specific forces (i.e., 1st Cavalry Division).

IV-29. Upon receipt of the JFLCC's requirements, the JFC works with the Service components to source the actual forces needed by the JFLCC. The Service components designate specific units to report to the JFC who assigns them to the JFLCC.

IV-30. Once the forces are designated, the JFC plans and conducts the strategic deployment of forces. While the JFLCC, like other functional components, provides recommended phasing of forces to the JFC, he will not control the land force portion of the TPFDD. Based on the Service and functional component recommendations, the JFC develops the integrated TPFDD and assigns the required delivery dates.

LIAISON, BOARD, AND CELL REQUIREMENTS

IV-31. Liaison teams or individuals should be dispatched from higher to lower, lower to higher, laterally, or any combination of these. The teams generally represent the interests of the sending commander to the gaining commander. However, they also promote understanding of the commander's intent at both the sending and gaining headquarters.

IV-32. The JFLCC liaison requirements include, as a minimum, liaison with other components of the joint force, the joint force headquarters, and major subordinate commands. The commander may require additional liaison with multinational land forces not assigned to the command.

Appendix A

Intelligence

GENERAL

A-1. The JFLCC is the JFC's focal point for adversary ground forces intelligence, target development, and battle damage assessment (BDA). He ensures required intelligence, surveillance, reconnaissance (ISR) support is provided to the JFC, functional components, and subordinate land component forces. Also, he defines intelligence responsibilities and prioritizes intelligence requirements of subordinate land forces. In addition, he provides representation for the land component and its subordinates at the JFC's daily joint coordination and targeting boards. The staff incorporates and synchronizes their human intelligence (HUMINT) and counterintelligence (CI) efforts with that of the commander-in-chief JTF J-2X.

A-2. The intelligence effort focuses on the integration of multisource information and multiechelon intelligence into all-source intelligence products. These products provide clear, relevant, and timely knowledge of the adversary and operational environment. The intelligence products and services must be in forms that are readily understood and usable by the recipient in a timely manner without overloading the user and, at the same time, minimizing the information management workload.

A-3. The JFLCC and his J-2 staff must understand the intelligence requirements of superior, subordinate, and component commands; identify organic intelligence capabilities and shortfalls; and access theater and national systems to ensure appropriate intelligence and CI products are provided or available.

A-4. The JFLCC J-2 is responsible for supporting the commander and staff by ensuring the availability of reliable intelligence and timely indications and warning on the characteristics of the area. The J-2 also ensures adequate intelligence collection and reporting to identify enemy capabilities and intentions as quickly as possible. Figure F-3, Appendix F, depicts a typical J-2 organization. The actual composition of the J-2 is dictated by the organization and operations to be conducted by the JFLCC. At a minimum, a core element of analytical, ISR management, and administrative capabilities is required.

A-5. J-2 responsibilities may include the following:

- Prioritizing the JFLC command intelligence requirements. This includes reviewing the CCIR to ensure that intelligence requirements for production, collection, and support to force protection are identified and processed.

- Ensuring the intelligence support to targeting and BDA is performed. This responsibility includes analyzing the adversary situation to identify, nominate, and assess those vulnerabilities that can be exploited by direct military operations. The J-2 provides appropriate targeting intelligence support, including target intelligence packages, to the JFLCC, JFACC, JTCB, and components.

- Developing concept-of-intelligence support operations to include intelligence and CI support to force protection.

- Executing intelligence battle handover. The J-2 follows established procedures for exchange of critical intelligence data

OFFICES, CENTERS, AND TEAMS

A-6. The joint analysis and control element (JACE) is the hub of intelligence production and ISR management in the JFLCC. The JACE is located at the JFLCC level and works directly for the J-2. This element is responsible for providing the complete ground adversary situation by integrating and adding to the combatant commander's intelligence organization. The JACE is formed from the Army Service component or corps analysis and control element or from the equivalent MAGTF intelligence support organization.

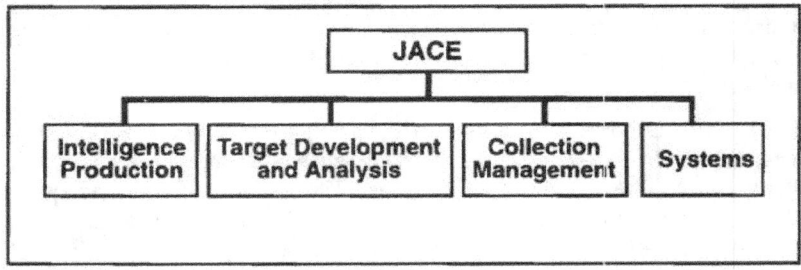

Figure A-1. Typical Joint Analysis and Control Element

A-7. The JACE is a tailored subset of the intelligence support organization providing intelligence support to JFLCC operational forces and performs common intelligence functions. By design, the JACE is scaleable and can expand to meet the needs of the JFLCC. It is tailored to fit the operating environment based on identified requirements.

A-8. The JACE is composed of analytical experts and analysis teams that provide services and products required by the commander, his staff, and components. These all-discipline and all-warfare specialty analysis teams are focused on substantive operational intelligence problems. Analysis teams take into account pertinent information from all sources. A JACE capability for all-source analysis and ISR management is key to operational intelligence.

A-9. Analytical efforts of the JACE should have an operational focus to help the commander better understand how the adversary plans, e.g., how he will conceptualize the situation, what his options are, and how he will react to a given situation.

A-10. During joint operations, CI and HUMINT complement each other and work together to provide intelligence and force protection support to the joint force. To accomplish this, the JFC establishes a joint force J-2 CI and HUMINT support element (J-2X) under the JFLCC. The J-2X manages, coordinates, and deconflicts HUMINT and CI activities of attached elements and Service components. The J-2X reports directly to the JFLCC J-2 and is responsible for the following:

- Task force CI coordinating authority (TFCICA) to coordinate CI force protection source operations, to maintain tactical source registry, to maintain liaison coordination, and to conduct CI collection management support functions.
- HUMINT operations cell (HOC) to coordinate operations, source administration, and requirements with the country team; establish liaison with the joint captured materiel exploitation center (JCMEC), joint document exploitation center (JDEC), joint interrogation and debriefing center (JIDC), and JACE; task HUMINT collection elements against identified priority enemy prisoners of war (EPWs), document, and foreign material acquisition requirements; and guide HUMINT operations toward elimination of intelligence gaps.

- Proper resource application to provide a coordinated, deconflicted, and integrated CI, HUMINT, and special operating forces (SOF) collection and reporting effort for the JFC and JFLCC.

A-11. While not all of the offices, centers, or teams listed below may be required, each should be evaluated based on future operations. The following may be established or requested by the JFLCC in addition to the J-2X and JACE:

- National Intelligence Support Team (NIST). NIST provides a mission-tailored national intelligence reach-back capability to fulfill the stated intelligence requirements of the supported JFLCC. Normally, it is composed of the Defense Intelligence Agency (DIA), Central Intelligence Agency, National Security Agency, National Imagery and Mapping Agency, and other intelligence resources as required. At a minimum, the personnel deployed in a NIST provide access to agency-unique information and supporting analysis.
- JCMEC. JCMEC is formed from elements of the DIA Foreign Materiel Program and service technical intelligence organizations and explosive ordnance disposal personnel. It is activated during periods of hostilities and assists in management of recovery, exploitation, and disposal of captured enemy equipment. This type of equipment can provide critical information on enemy strengths and weaknesses that may favorably influence operational planning.
- Joint Interrogation Facility (JIF). JIF conducts initial screening and interrogation of EPWs, translation and exploitation of captured adversary documents, and debriefing of captured or detained US personnel released or escaped from adversary control. It coordinates exploitation of captured equipment with the JCMEC, documents with the JDEC, and human sources with the JIDC. The JIF forwards key reports to the JIDC. More than one JIF may be established in the JOA depending upon the anticipated number of EPWs.
- JIDC. JIDC conducts follow-on exploitation of EPWs. EPWs are screened by the JIFs, and those of further intelligence potential are identified and forwarded to the JIDC for follow-on interrogation and debriefing in support of JTF and higher requirements. Besides EPWs, the JIDC may also interrogate civilian detainees, refugees, and other nonprisoner sources. JIDC activities are managed by the J-2X HOC. The HOC coordinates with the TFCICA for CI augmentation for

exploitation of those personnel of CI interest, such as civil and/or military leaders, intelligence and political officers, and terrorists.

- JDEC. The JDEC exploits captured adversary documents and other media to obtain intelligence. Document exploitation can obtain information on topics, such as information on adversary intentions and planning (including deception), locations, dispositions, tactics, communications, logistics, and morale. Coupled with other intelligence sources, document exploitation provides a more complete picture of an unfolding operation and adversary capabilities. The JDEC is activated during periods of hostilities, deployed to the COCOM, and normally assigned to, and under the OPCON of, the JFLCC J-2 to manage the recovery, exploitation, automated processing, and disposal of captured adversary documents.

A-12. More detailed discussions of ISR operations and considerations are found in the JP 2-0 series on intelligence.

Appendix B

Movement and Maneuver

GENERAL

B-1. The JFLCC plans, controls, and coordinates land movement and maneuver to gain a positional advantage or a mobility differential over the adversary. The purpose is to achieve the objectives assigned in the JFC campaign plan.

B-2. JP 3-0 describes maneuver at the operational level as a means by which commanders set the terms of battle by time and location, decline battle, or exploit existing situations. The objective for operational maneuver is usually a COG or decisive point.

KEY CONSIDERATIONS

B-3. The JFLCC assumes control of the forces from the Service component upon completion of their reception, staging, onward movement, and integration in theater. He must have the requisite C^2 capability to effectively employ the force.

B-4. One key difference between a JFLCC and a Service component commander is the requirement for the JFLCC to effectively integrate the different capabilities, requirements, and limitations of the forces assigned to accomplish the assigned mission.

B-5. The notional JFLC command headquarters, discussed in Appendix F, provides for the integration of staff officers from each Service into each section of the JFLC command staff. It is essential that officers from each Service participate in the planning process of all movement and maneuver to insure Service-unique capabilities and limitations are considered.

B-6. A key to maximizing capabilities is to understand the battlespace requirements of each assigned force. An example is the requirement to provide the MAGTF with sufficient battlespace (either linear or nonlinear AO) to effectively employ its air combat element. This requires detailed and continuous coordination with the JFACC and careful consideration of FSCMs and boundaries.

B-7. The JFC normally tasks the JFLCC to make recommendations on the employment of forces. This includes the following:

- Organizing for combat.
- Integrating multinational land forces in the land fight.
- Developing a land force scheme of maneuver and fire support plan to support the JFC's campaign plan.
- Identifying interdiction targets or objectives within the JFLCC's boundaries. He should clearly state how interdiction enhances or enables his maneuver operations.
- Establishing priorities of effort.
- Designating the fire support coordination lines and internal boundaries.
- Coordinating/integrating/synchronizing operational reconnaissance.
- Coordinating/planning operational fires that impact maneuver.

Appendix C

Administration and Logistics

GENERAL

C-1. Joint administrative functions include personnel, pay input, religion, and legal support services (see JP 1-series publications).

C-2. The six logistics functions are defined in joint doctrine as: supply, maintenance, health services, transportation, services, and general engineering. (See JP 4-0 and other JP 4-series publications.)

DIRECTIVE AUTHORITY
FOR LOGISTICS

C-3. In joint operations, the geographical combatant commander, through the subordinate JFCs, Service components, and DOD agencies (primarily Defense Logistics Agency), ensures effective and efficient execution of personnel and logistics services consistent with the overall campaign plan. (See Figure C-1.) The exercise of directive authority for logistics by a combatant commander includes the authority to issue directives to subordinate commanders, including peacetime measures, necessary to ensure the execution of approved OPLANs, the effectiveness and economy of operation, and the prevention or elimination of unnecessary duplication of facilities and overlapping functions among the Service component commands.

C-4. A combatant commander's limited directive authority for logistics is not intended to—

- Usurp Service responsibility for logistics support.
- Discourage coordination by consultation and agreement.
- Disrupt effective procedures, efficient use of facilities, or organization.

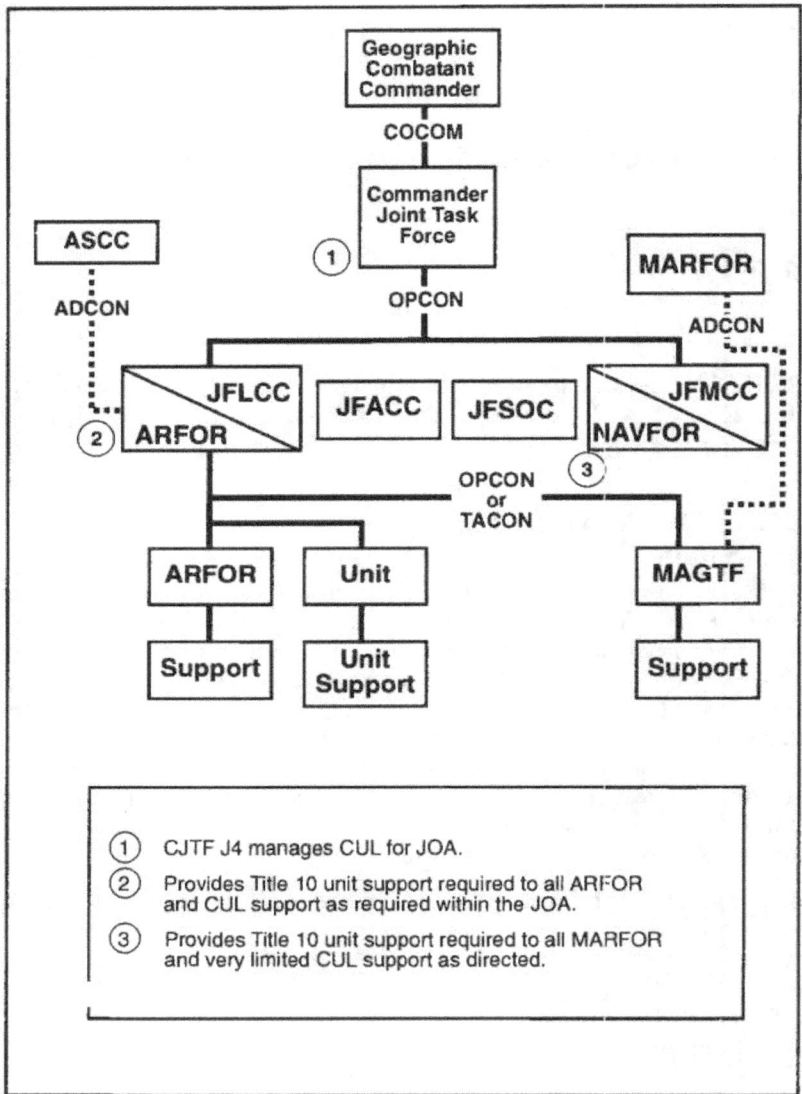

Figure C-1. Example of Logistics Authority with ARFOR Designated as JFLCC

COMMON USER LOGISTICS

C-5. The JFC develops the overarching campaign plan in concert with the combatant commander's guidance and with input from subordinate Service component commands, functional component commands, and DOD agencies. In concert with the JFC planning effort, the JFLCC develops the land operations portion of the campaign plan. This land OPLAN is provided to the JFC for consideration in developing and coordinating deployment and employment of forces and support of the overall campaign plan. The individual Service component commands, however, have overall responsibility for providing logistics support to their own forces unless otherwise directed. (See JP 4-07.)

C-6. Service component forces, especially the Army, are often required to provide significant levels of JOA-wide common user logistics (CUL) support to other Service components, multinational partners, and other organizations (i.e., other governmental organizations [OGOs]) and NGOs. Army JOA-wide CUL support requirements are normally provided by Army echelon-above-corps support units, such as the theater support command, but these requirements are carried out under the auspices of the ARFOR commander and are not a JFLCC responsibility. (See FM 100-10 and FM 63-4 for further information.) The MARFOR may provide limited CUL support to other Service component forces based on the plan.

C-7. In some cases, the JFLCC may direct selected CUL support within his AO; however, the authority to direct logistics is not resident in the JFLCC's OPCON or TACON authority (see JP 0-2, page III-8). When required, JFLCC CUL authority may be derived from one of two sources: combatant commander delegation of specific land-operation-focused CUL authority or through short-term interservice support agreements between the ARFOR and MARFOR.

C-8. With this limited CUL authority, the JFLCC may direct that CUL support be provided between the Service component units. This land-operations-focused CUL may include temporary task organization or support relationships of selected JFLCC logistics units. (Land-operations-focused CUL support is separate and distinct from JOA-wide CUL requirements.) The JFLCC J-4 staff ensures that JFLCC-directed CUL requirements do not conflict or interfere with combatant-commander-directed JOA-wide CUL requirements.

LOGISTICS PLANNING

C-9. JFLCC logistics plans should be integrated with combatant commander annexes and JFC, Service component, and multinational partner logistics plans.

C-10. JFLCC J-4 personnel must be involved early in the staff planning and undertake an analysis of the logistics support capabilities of each of the COAs considered.

C-11. JFLCC CUL requirements must be properly planned and coordinated with overall combatant commander/JFC-directed CUL requirements.

C-12. JFLCC J-4 personnel determine location and accessibility of key supply points.

C-13. The JFLCC J-4 planners identify those issues unique to the land operations not already identified by the JFC J-4 reports.

BOARDS
AND CENTERS

C-14. The JFLCC is not routinely the lead for JFC-level logistics boards and centers. The JFLCC J-4 normally participates in selected combatant commander/JFC boards and centers that are of critical importance to the successful execution of the land campaign. The joint transportation board and the joint movement center are transportation-related boards and centers that may have significant impact on the land portion of the joint campaign and are examples of higher level joint logistics boards on which the JFLCC may want representation. Other boards and centers of significant importance to the JFC include the joint material priorities and allocation board and the joint petroleum office. To ensure proper focus, the JFLCC participation in these boards needs to be treated as separate and distinct from the Service component participation in these same boards and centers. (See Figure C-2.)

Possible Joint Logistics Boards and Centers

- Joint Transportation Board
- Joint Movement Center
- Joint Petroleum Office
- Joint Civil-Military Engineering Board
- Joint Facilities Utilization Board
- Theater Patient Movement Requirements Center
- Joint Blood Program Office
- Joint Mortuary Affairs Office
- Joint Material Priorities and Allocation Board

Figure C-2 Joint Logistics Boards and Centers

C-15. The JFLCC will not normally convene separate joint logistics boards and centers except when needed to coordinate critical CUL support within the JFLCC AO. Possible JFLCC-established boards and centers may include a movement center and materials priorities allocation board (MPAB). The movement center facilitates coordination and prioritization of movement within the JFLCC's AO. The movement center would be subordinate to the JFC joint movement center and would ensure that JFLCC movement requirements do not conflict with JFC-directed movements. The JFLCC-level joint movement center would be built on the lead Service movement control agency and include staff members from the other Service. A JFLCC MPAB would perform similar functions for critical supply items. (The JFLCC could combine these two centers/boards into one distribution management center that would perform both transportation and supply management functions.) In any case, he will ensure that he has the capability to adequately control movement and cross-level critical logistics resources when necessary for execution of land operations.

FUNCTIONS
OF THE J-1 AND J-4

C-16. The JFLCC J-1 and J-4 provide critical functional expertise to the commander in the areas of personnel and logistics. These primary staff officers focus on key personnel and logistics issues that may have an adverse affect on the land portion of the joint campaign.

C-17. Generally, they manage by exception only. Routine administrative/personnel and logistics management is the responsibility of the JFC and the subordinate Service component commands. See Appendix F for more information on JFLCC J-1 and J-4 staff organization and responsibilities.

Appendix D

Firepower

GENERAL

D-1. This appendix provides information regarding JFLC command fires, to include the targeting process, organization, and the planning and execution of fires at the operational level and assessment of the effects of those fires.

FIRES MISSION

D-2. The JFLCC and his staff plan and execute operational fires to accomplish the mission and create the conditions for success on the battlefield.

D-3. The JFLCC uses fires as the principle means of shaping the battlespace. His interests are those theaterwide adversary forces, functions, facilities, and operations that impact on future land force plans and operations. He focuses on adversary operational (and limited strategic) level COGs, using joint and combined lethal and nonlethal means, to shape the operational battlefield to achieve a decisive impact on the conduct of the campaign or major operation. The JFLCC generally has three primary goals when conducting operational fires:

- Facilitating both operational and tactical maneuver by suppressing the adversary's deep-strike systems, disrupting the adversary's operational maneuver and tempo, and creating exploitable gaps in adversary positions.
- Isolating the battlespace by interdicting adversary military potential before it can be used effectively against friendly forces.
- Destroying critical adversary functions and facilities that eliminate or substantially degrade adversary operational capabilities.

RESOURCES

D-4. The JFLCC employs fires through joint and organic resources.

D-5. The JFLCC's primary tools to attack operational targets (OP.2.2, Appendix H) are operational fires and joint interdiction. Interdiction is defined as actions to divert, disrupt, delay, or destroy the adversary's surface military potential before it can be used effectively against friendly forces. Joint resources for interdiction include:

- Air.
- SOF.
- National/theater/JTF offensive IO.
- Army attack helicopters.
- Army Tactical Missile System (ATACMS).

TARGETING

D-6. Targeting occurs at all levels of command within a joint force and is applied by Service and component-level forces capable of attacking targets with lethal and nonlethal means to achieve the desired effects. Components must understand the joint targeting process to fulfill the JFLCC's intent and objectives. Effective coordination, deconfliction, and synchronization maximize the strategic, operational, and tactical effects of joint targeting. Components must have effective joint targeting procedures that ensure:

- Compliance with JFLCC's objectives, guidance, and intent.
- Coordination, synchronization, and deconfliction of attacks.
- Rapid response to time-sensitive targets (TSTs).
- Minimal duplication of effort.
- Expeditious effects assessment.
- Common perspective of all targeting efforts.
- Fratricide avoidance.

D-7. Decisions to modify missions or direct attacks that deviate from the planned activity must be based on the commander's guidance. These decisions are made with the understanding of the perspective and target priorities of other component targeting efforts throughout the campaign. Some priority targets may present themselves at the worst possible time for the accomplishment of the campaign plan.

JOINT TARGETING PROCESS FUNCTIONS AND RESPONSIBILITIES

D-8. The JFLCC conducts the joint targeting process within an established organizational framework. A primary consideration in organizing this framework is the joint force's ability to coordinate, deconflict, and synchronize joint targeting operations.

D-9. The structure established by the JFLCC facilitates the joint targeting process. The JFLCC defines this structure based on the JFC's requirements, the capabilities of assigned, attached, and supporting forces, as well as the adversary, mission, and operational area. In addition, it must react to rapidly changing events. Likewise, it should execute all phases of the joint targeting process efficiently and continuously. (See JP 3-60 for more information.)

FIRES SYNCHRONIZATION AND COORDINATION

D-10. The JFLCC accomplishes fires synchronization and coordination through the J-3 in the deep operations coordination cell (DOCC) or force fires coordination center (FFCC). The functions and responsibilities of the DOCC or FFCC are as follows:

- Advise on application of operational fires/effects.
- Identify fires effects requirements from other components (air interdiction/naval surface fire support).
- Review and comment on the JFACC's apportionment recommendation.
- Recommend JFLCC assets for JFC allocation (ATACMS/attack helicopter).
- Advise on fires asset distribution (priority) to land forces.
- Develop JFLCC priorities, timing, and effects for air interdiction within the JFLCC AO.
- Develop JFLCC targeting guidance and priorities.
- Develop the JFLC command target lists and FSCMs.
- Plan, coordinate, and supervise the execution of JFLCC deep operations.
- Integrate and synchronize lethal and nonlethal fires.
- Coordinate with Army airspace command and control (A^2C^2) cell for all planned airspace requirements.

D-11. Targets requiring immediate response because they pose a clear and present danger to friendly forces, or are highly lucrative, fleeting targets of opportunity are known as TSTs.

D-12. The fire support element (FSE) may establish a quick-fire net for the coordination of locating and striking TSTs. This may be by radio, phone conference call, or computer chatter link. As a minimum, this net links the DOCC/FFCC, collection management, and the battlefield coordination detachment (BCD). Additional nodes may be a major subordinate command (MSC) FSE, Army Air Missile Defense Command (AAMDC), special staff, J-3 current operations, and others as the situation dictates.

D-13. The quick-fire procedures, by definition, state targets submitted are of critical need. In the event an MSC has a quick-fire request, it may initiate a call on the quick-fire net. The request is evaluated on the basis of need, criticality, and comparison with other targets. If the MSC does not receive timely response or the request is denied, the DOCC/FFCC chief adjudicates the request.

D-14. All TST requirements must be forwarded directly to/handled by the FSE. Any section in receipt of TSTs will follow through until the requirement is handed over to the FSE.

D-15. The joint targeting process cuts across traditional functional and organizational boundaries. Operations, plans, and intelligence are the primary active participants, but other functional areas such as logistics, weather, law, and communications may also support the joint targeting process. Close coordination, cooperation, and communication are essential. The JFLCC develops guidance that directs and focuses operation planning and targeting to support the CONOPS.

TARGETING COORDINATION BOARD

D-16. Typically, JFLCCs organize a targeting coordination board (TCB) to function as an integrating center to accomplish targeting oversight functions or as a JFLCC-level review mechanism. In either case, it needs to be a joint activity with representatives from the JFLC command staff, all components, and subordinate units.

D-17. JFLC command TCB responsibilities are—

- To retain authority and responsibility to direct target priorities, relative level of subordinate unit effort, and sequence of those efforts of his subordinate units.

- To provide clear guidance and objectives for operational planning and targeting.
- To update mission planning guidance, intent, and priority intelligence requirements throughout the targeting process.
- To direct the formation, composition, and specific responsibilities of a TCB.

D-18. JFLC command staff TCB responsibilities (overall) are—

- To provide a forum for review of the joint targeting guidance and apportionment.
- To advise the JFLCC on the plan to achieve overall theater plans and objectives.
- To assist all subordinate units in translating JFLCC objectives and guidance into coordinated subordinate operations and plans.
- To provide COAs in the form of board targeting guidance based on the major OPLANs and priorities.
- To review the JFLCC major OPLANs several days in advance and to act as an advisory board to the JFLCC to anticipate future operations in his major operation. The TCB is a valuable vehicle to help the JFLCC—
  - Coordinate targeting information.
  - Develop targeting guidance and priorities.
  - Define the desired effects of joint targeting.
  - Recommend supplemental ROEs.
  - Review target information.
  - Recommend changes to the JFC's restricted and no-strike target lists.
- To compile subordinate targeting nominations/requirements and prioritize targets based on JFLCC guidance.
- To develop the candidate target list (CTL) for JFLCC approval.

D-19. Intelligence directorate (J-2) responsibilities are—

- To provide intelligence support to joint targeting.
- To provide coordination of ISR resources, reporting, products, and services to support the JFLCC's targeting requirements.

- To recommend collection priorities for JFC, theater, and national tasking and to work with the J-3 to support collection requirements.

- To conduct CA and evaluate effectiveness of nonlethal operations to provide CA to the J-3.

D-20. Operations and plans directorates (J-3/J-5) responsibilities are—

- To ensure the J-2 has the required information/priorities for target development, target acquisition, and CA.

- To coordinate closely with the J-2 organic collection efforts.

- To develop effects assessments for the JFLCC with support from the staff and each subordinate and other functional components.

- To manage the TCB and related boards, including CA board and IO working group and to provide TCB meeting results to each subordinate unit and supporting forces.

D-21. Offensive IO responsibilities are—

- To coordinate IO defensive and offensive concepts and to establish priorities to accomplish IO objectives to support the JFLCC's intent and CONOPS.

- To determine the availability of resources to carry out IO plan and to coordinate intelligence and assessment support to IO.

- To serve as the primary advocate for offensive IO (lethal and nonlethal) targets nominated for attack throughout the target nomination and review process established by the JFLCC.

D-22. Logistics directorate (J-4) responsibilities are—

- To identify critical or key logistics issues unique to specific JFLCC operations.

- To recommend logistics priorities for JFLCC taskings and identify logistics shortfalls.

- To identify enemy logistics targets, (i.e., fuel storage depots and pipelines, distribution infrastructure, and hubs to include both airports and seaports) that would affect their capability to wage war.

- To review target selection for unnecessary adverse environmental impacts (i.e., dams, oil fields, etc.).

D-23. Staff judge advocate responsibilities are to advise the TCB on applicable international and domestic laws, Law of Armed Conflict issues, ROEs, and other pertinent issues involved in target recommendations and decisions processes.

D-24. Subordinate unit responsibilities are—

- To identify requirements and nominate targets to the JFLCC.
- To provide LNO team to include representation to the TCB.
- To recommend priorities for BDA collection requirements to the JFLCC J-2.

COMPONENT TARGET COORDINATION RESPONSIBILITIES

D-25. The JFACC/JFC staff develops a joint air operations plan to accomplish the objectives directed by the JFC. Synchronization, integration, deconfliction, allocation of air capabilities/forces, and matching appropriate weapons against target vulnerabilities are essential targeting functions for the JFACC. Other components targeting requirements to support their assigned missions are provided to the JFC and JFACC for sourcing in attack. Therefore, targets scheduled for deliberate attack by subordinate direct support air capabilities/forces should be included in the joint air tasking order (ATO), when appropriate, for deconfliction and coordination.

D-26. All component commanders within the joint force should have a basic understanding of each component's mission and general CONOPS/scheme of maneuver to support the JFC's campaign plan. Therefore, the JFLCC provides the JFACC a description of the direct support plan through the liaison elements (BCD/Marine LNO) within the joint air operations center. This basic understanding allows for coordination and deconfliction of targeting efforts between each component and within the JFC staff and agencies.

D-27. Once guidance is received from higher headquarters, the target nomination process begins with the deliberate targeting process. This may include the following:

- Long-term planning guidance, the commander's intent for fires, and other component guidance for coordination and situational awareness.
- Receipt of MSC guidance and intent for incorporation into the JFLCC's targeting guidance.
- The JFLCC's intent as provided in OPORDS, OPLANS, operations planning group information, and, most importantly, direct guidance.

D-28. The DOCC/FFCC presents guidance, objectives, and tasks (3 days out) to the daily targeting board (DTB) for approval or modification by the deputy JFLCC. These approved guidance, objectives, and tasks are provided to MSCs for review, comment, and to provide basis for specific target nominations and to the DOCC/FFCC target development for input to draft CTL.

D-29. To create the CTL, DOCC/FFCC targeting receives the MSCs target nominations in accordance with the target objectives distributed from the DTB. MSC nominations and JFLCC pre-planned targets are combined to form the JFLCC prioritized list of targets. Targets nominations are then checked for CA, projected locations (mobile targets), and reviewed by objective and task to ensure consistency with the approved guidance. The next step is the CTL review board. This board is attended by representatives from the MSCs, the DOCC/FFCC chief, DOCC/FFCC targeting and operations, the staff judge advocate, and other staff elements as needed. This process allows the MSCs to gain visibility on their nominated targets. It also allows for review of targets by the staff judge advocate for law-of-land warfare compliance and no-strike list conflicts. The approved CTL is then forwarded to the BCD. The BCD then compares the CTL against JFLCC's priorities for inclusion in ATO development.

AIR TASKING ORDER

D-30. An ATO is critical to the JFLCC. The ATO is the primary means of shaping the operational level fight.

D-31. The DOCC/FFCC receives the ATO daily via the contingency theater automated planning system/theater battle management core system. Upon receipt of the ATO, the DOCC/FFCC completes the following tasks:

- Scrubs the ATO for non-JFLCC targets scheduled within the JFLCC AO. If necessary, deconflicts JFLCC deep operations plan accordingly. Notifies the JFACC through the BCD/Marine LNO of any planned targets that would adversely impact the JFLCC's operation.
- Highlights JFLCC targets from the CTL that made the ATO.
- Highlights JFLCC component targets on the ATO.
- Prepares the divert list to cover essential targets that did not make the ATO.
- Prepares the ATO book containing critical information pertaining to the next day's ATO such as supported target list, ATO divert list, CTL, ATO, battlespace shaping matrix, and special instructions.

D-32. To ensure complete information transfer, DOCC/FFCC conducts an ATO handover briefing for the next day's ATO with current operations FSE. This handover book covers—

- Situation update.
- Target guidance/objectives.
- CTL overview (number targets nominated, brief target overlay).
- ATO overview (number CTL targets supported, number CTL targets nonsupported, ATO divert sheet, divert/re-role guidance and directives, and CAS distribution.
- Current situation.
- Significant friendly situation (allocation of weight of effort of the ATO, high payoff target list, fire support coordination line changes, and weather impacts).

EFFECTS ASSESSMENT

D-33. Effects assessment addresses the effectiveness of overall joint targeting in light of the JFLCC's objectives, guidance, and intent. It gives the JFLCC and the JFC a broad perspective of the total effect of joint targeting against the enemy at the operational and strategic levels. The effects assessment attempts to answer the following questions:

- Are combat operations (lethal and nonlethal) achieving mission objectives?
- Do objectives require modification?
- How effective was targeting in terms of impacting the enemy's warfighting capabilities?
- What specific changes in combat operations would improve friendly efforts to degrade the adversary's will and capability to conduct operations?
- Has an adversary target system increased or decreased in importance based on furture combat operations?
- Were there any unanticipated operational limitations?

D-34. The effects assessment is determined during the combat assessment board (CAB). The CAB is an action officer forum used by the commander to determine the overall effectiveness of force employment, fires, and maneuver to achieve commander's objectives. CA is composed of three major components—

- BDA.
- Munitions effects assessment.
- Re-attack recommendations.

D-35. The objective of the CAB is to identify and measure the effectiveness of joint actions and recommend courses of action. Some of the areas covered in the CAB include—

- Current friendly and advesary 24-48-hour picture.
- A 72-hour outlook to ensure targeting is tied to current mission effectiveness.
- Spot reports, mission reports, and CA by target objective.
- Recommended targets for re-strike and recommended changes to targeting objectives and guidance.

D-36. The following is a sample of CAB members:

- J-2 operations and plans.
- Intelligence production, CA, and collection management.
- J-3 current operations, future operations and plans.
- J-3 DOCC/FFCC operations and target development.
- J-3 FSE.
- J-3 IO.
  - Coordinates the overall IO effort for the JFLCC.
  - Coordinates IO inputs from joint centers and agencies and coordinates liaison with outside organizations such as the joint information operations center and land information warfare activity.
  - Conducts and coordinates IO working group meetings with the seven elements (operational security, psychological operations, electronic warfare (EW), civil affairs, public affairs, military deception, and physical destruction; provides IO working group meeting results to the DTB and JFLCC staff.
- J-4 operations.
- J-7 engineers.
- AAMDC.
- MSC LNOs.
- Joint warfare analysis center.
- Land information warfare agency.

Appendix E

Force Protection

GENERAL

E-1. Force protection is a responsibility of command, not a separate mission. The JFLCC must consider all elements associated with meeting this requirement. This appendix provides additional clarity for theater air and missile defense (TAMD) operations and other force protection issues. Outside the context of AT, force protection includes actions taken to prevent or mitigate hostile actions against DOD personnel (to include family members), resources, facilities, and critical information. These actions conserve the force's fighting potential so it can be applied at the decisive time and place and incorporate the coordinated and synchronized offensive and defensive measures to enable the effective employment of the joint force while degrading opportunities for the enemy.

E-2. Force protection does not include actions to defeat the enemy or protect against accidents, weather, or disease. Figure E-1 depicts elements of force protection.

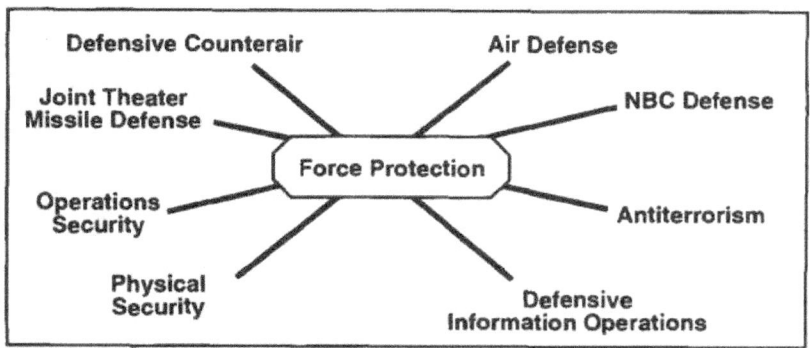

Figure E-1. Elements of Force Protection

THEATER AIR AND MISSILE DEFENSE

E-3. The JFLCC ensures that TAMD operations conducted by land forces are planned, coordinated, and synchronized with the other components within the theater of operations. The JFLCC may employ the AAMDC to perform these functions. The AAMDC is an Army C^2 headquarters tailored for joint operations and is capable of planning, coordinating, and synchronizing TAMD operations, including the theater missile defense (TMD) operational elements of active defense, passive defense, attack operations, and C^4 intelligence.

E-4. The commander of the AAMDC performs three critical roles during TAMD operations. The commander commands the AAMDC and its subordinate echelon-above-corps ADA brigades, performs the functions of the theater Army air and missile defense coordinator (TAAMDCOORD) for the ARFOR (or JFLCC, if appointed), and performs the function of DAADC for the JFACC/area air defense commander (AADC).

E-5. The TAAMDCOORD, as a special staff officer to the ARFOR commander or JFLCC, ensures Army/land-based air and missile defense (AMD) is integrated with the joint and multinational active air defense operations and planning at the theater level. The TAAMDCOORD recommends air and missile threats as offensive counterair and DCA priorities to the ARFOR commander/JFLCC, who in turn reviews and forwards these recommendations to the JFACC/AADC.

E-6. The DAADC provides the following TAMD support to the AADC:

- Integrates land-based AMD and DCA.
- Assists the AADC with the area air defense plan development.
- Advises the AADC on ROEs, airspace control measures, weapon control measures, and air defense warnings.
- Advises the AADC on land-based AMD operations and capabilities.

E-7. The AAMDC normally collocates with the ARFOR/JFLCC headquarters, but dependent on mission, enemy, terrain and weather, troops and support available, time available, and civilians (METT-TC), may collocate with the joint air operations center. The location of the commander and his role is also dependent on METT-TC. The commander is supported in the TAMD mission by AAMDC liaison teams that may deploy to all major theater C^2 headquarters including the JFLCC, JFACC/AADC, JFMCC, and to the ARFOR elements of the DOCC, BCD, and aviation control element.

E-8. For additional guidance on AMD, refer to JP 3-01 and JP 3-01.5.

NUCLEAR, BIOLOGICAL, AND CHEMICAL DEFENSE

E-9. NBC defense measures protect against attack by NBC weapons and provide the capability to sustain operations in NBC environments using the principles of avoidance of NBC hazards, particularly contamination, protection of individuals and units from unavoidable NBC hazards, and decontamination.

E-10. Commanders at all levels are responsible for the following:

- Ensuring all personnel are proficient in the individual and collective NBC defense skills required to carry out their respective missions in an NBC environment.
- Conducting collective training designed to ensure units can execute their mission-essential tasks in an NBC environment.
- Providing chemical defense equipment (CDE) to units and individuals. At the minimum, ensure individuals and units have adequate stocks of protection, detection, and decontamination equipment. Commanders should continuously monitor CDE stocks to ensure they do not fall below minimum levels established by the JFLCC.
- Implementing the Nuclear, Biological, and Chemical Warning and Reporting System.
- In accordance with the policy of each service, maintaining a well-trained core of NBC defense specialists and service-specific NBC defense infrastructure prepared to assist units to operate effectively in an NBC environment.
- Providing NBC intelligence to higher, adjacent, subordinate, and attached units.
- Developing and implementing automatic procedures for the verification of enemy use of NBC. Being prepared to provide next higher headquarters with verification of enemy first use of NBC weapons in their AO.
- Developing and implementing NBC reconnaissance and decontamination plans. Being prepared to develop and implement smoke plans in the event smoke generator units are placed in support of unit operations.

E-11. Personnel having staff responsibility for NBC defense matters at all levels within each component will—

- Advise the commander and staff on all aspects of NBC operations.
- Provide input on all plans and orders.
- Prepare, receive, collect, evaluate, and distribute NBC reports.

E-12. The NBC threat warning system is employed by the JFLCC to provide component commanders with information from which they can establish appropriate unit defense measures. This system consolidates the most current intelligence estimates regarding the enemy's offensive capabilities, intent, and activities, and recommends measures to be employed to combat this threat.

- The JFLCC J-3 establishes the NBC THREATCON in coordination with the J-2 and JFLCC NBC defense point of contact. Once established, the THREATCON is disseminated via J-2 and J-3 channels.
- Actions associated with each THREATCON are recommended, not directive in nature. They are based on current NBC defense doctrine but should be assessed in context of the unit's situation and mission.
- NBC THREATCONs are not synonymous with the mission-oriented protective posture (MOPP) levels. Threat is only one of the factors commanders consider when determining the appropriate MOPP level.

E-13. The JFLCC, in coordination with and approval from the JFC, establishes close relationships with US departments and agencies within their sphere of C^2. Networks are established with diplomatic missions and country teams within the AO. These sources may provide valuable intelligence on the likelihood of enemy intent to introduce NBC weapons. They may also produce data on the political and psychological implications, as well as military aspects of effectively countering NBC weapons beyond that provided by intelligence sources subordinate to the JFLCC.

E-14. For additional guidance on NBC defense, refer to JP 3-11.

ANTITERRORISM MEASURES

E-15. In AT, force protection is the security program designed to protect Service members, civilian employees, family members, facilities, and equipment, in all locations and situations. This is accomplished through planned and integrated application of combating terrorism, physical security, operations security (OPSEC), and personal protective services and is supported by CI and other security programs.

E-16. To meet the terrorist threat, an integrated and comprehensive JFLCC AT program must be developed and implemented. AT measures are intended to identify and reduce the risk of loss or damage of potential targets and to develop procedures to detect and deter planned terrorist actions before they take place, thereby reducing the probability of a terrorist event. The measures also encompass the reactive or tactical stage of an incident, including direct contact with terrorists to end the incident with minimum loss of life and property. For assets under the control of the JFLCC, an appropriate division of responsibilities is coordinated with the JFC.

E-17. The AT program stresses deterrence of terrorist incidents through preventive measures. The program addresses the following:

- Threat analysis.
- Installation or unit criticality and vulnerability assessments.
- Threat assessment based on the threat analysis and friendly vulnerabilities.
- Information security.
- OPSEC.
- Personnel security.
- Physical security.
- Crisis management planning.
- Employment of tactical measures to contain or resolve terrorist incidents.
- Continuous training and education of personnel.
- Public affairs planning.

E-18. For additional guidance on AT, refer to JP 3-07.2.

DEFENSIVE INFORMATION OPERATIONS

E-19. Defensive IO integrate and coordinate protection and defense of information and information systems (which include C^4 systems, sensors, weapon systems, infrastructure systems, and decision-makers). Defensive IO is an integral part of overall force protection. Defensive IO is conducted through information assurance, physical security, OPSEC, counter-deception, counter-psychological operations, CI, EW, and special information operations. Defense IO personnel coordinate defense IO objectives to support the JFLCC's intent and concept of operations.

E-20. Four interrelated processes comprise defensive IO—

- Information environment protection.
- Attack detection.
- Capability restoration.
- Attack response.

E-21. The JFLCC is responsible for effectively integrating defensive IO. An IO officer should be designated. This officer or an assistant interfaces with the joint force IO cell to provide component expertise and acts as a liaison for IO matters between the joint force and the component. This representative also may serve as a member of one or more of the supporting organizations of IO (e.g., the special technical operations cell).

E-22. For additional guidance on defensive IO, refer to JP 3-13.

PHYSICAL SECURITY MEASURES

E-23. Physical security measures deter, detect, and defend against threats from terrorists, criminals, and unconventional forces. Measures include fencing and perimeter standoff space, lighting and sensors, vehicle barriers, blast protection, intrusion detection systems and electronic surveillance, and access control devices and systems.

E-24. Physical security measures, like any defense, should be overlapping and deployed in depth.

E-25. For additional guidance on physical security measures, refer to JP 3-10 and JP 3-10.1.

OPERATIONS SECURITY MEASURES

E-26. Effective OPSEC measures minimize the *signature* of JFLCC activities, avoid set patterns, and employ deception when patterns cannot be altered. Although strategic OPSEC measures are important, the most effective methods manifest themselves at the lowest level.

E-27. Terrorist activity is discouraged by varying patrol routes, staffing guard posts and towers at irregular intervals, and conducting vehicle and personnel searches and identification checks on a set but unpredictable pattern.

E-28. Law enforcement aids in force protection through the prevention, detection, response, and investigation of crime. A cooperative police program involving military and civilian/host-nation law enforcement agencies directly contributes to overall force protection.

E-29. Personnel security measures range from general measures of AT to specialized personal protective services. They include commonsense rules of on- and off-duty conduct, use of protective clothing and equipment, use of hardened vehicles and facilities, employment of dedicated guard forces, and use of duress alarms.

E-30. For additional guidance on OPSEC, refer to JP 3-54.

PLANNING

E-31. The JFLCC must address force protection during all phases of deliberate and crisis action planning. All aspects of force protection must be considered and threats minimized to ensure maximum operational success. The JFLCC and subordinate commanders must implement force protection measures appropriate to anticipated terrorist threats.

E-32. Supported and supporting commanders must ensure that deploying forces receive thorough briefings concerning the threat and personnel protection requirements prior to and upon arrival in the theater of operations.

E-33. In addition, the JFLCC and subordinate commanders must evaluate the deployment of forces and each COA for the impact of terrorist organizations supporting the threat and those not directly supporting the threat but seeking to take advantage of the situation.

E-34. For additional guidance on force protection and related matters and considerations, refer to risk management and OPSEC guidance in JP 3-07.2.

Notional Headquarters Organization

GENERAL

F-1. The JFLC command staff is organized based upon the mission and forces assigned. Since formation of a new headquarters would be very time consuming and inefficient, the staff organization will most likely be based upon an existing command element. The most likely candidates are an Army corps, a MAGTF (most likely a MEF), Army or Marine Service component command or, when separately constituted, a numbered army.

F-2. Augmentees from the other Services are integrated into the core staff to form the JFLC command staff. Ideally, the JFLCC and his deputy would come from different Services. This construct should be replicated throughout the staff leadership to ensure an understanding of the distinct capabilities of each Service to optimize employment of the forces. Figure F-1 depicts a notional staff organization.

STAFF

F-3. While Figure F-1 depicts a notional staff organization, it is not prescriptive. The practical assumption is that the actual staff organization is based on the staff organization of the corps, MAGTF, or army that forms the core of the staff with some staff members being dual-hatted. Therefore, the actual location of certain sections (i.e., engineer) and the specific special staff vary according to the organization of the core staff and METT-T.

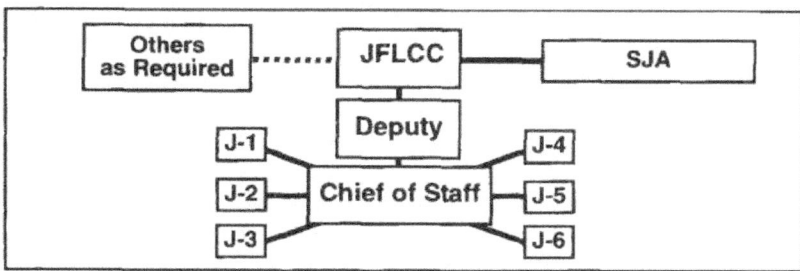

Figure F-1. Notional JFLCC Organization

STAFF RESPONSIBILITIES

F-4. The J-1 is the principal staff assistant for personnel service support and personnel administration. The majority of personnel and administrative actions is handled via the Service component G-1 through the JFC J-1. The JFC J-1 is responsible for monitoring current and projected unit strengths by daily personnel status, casualty, and critical reports of personnel shortages. The JFC J-1 analyzes these reports and determines any effects they would have on land operations. These reports would be routinely provided from the ARFOR and MARFOR G-1s to the JFC with copy furnished to the JFLCC J-1. Note: The JFLCC J-1 is not in the formal personnel reporting chain. A notional J-1 organization is provided in Figure F-2.

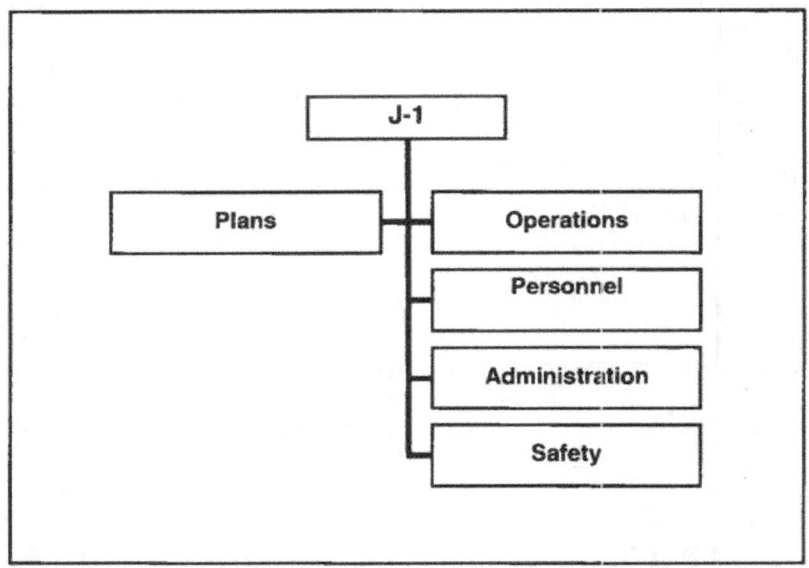

Figure F-2. Notional JFLCC J-1 Staff Section

F-5. The primary role of the J-2 is to provide intelligence support to the JFLCC. A notional organization of the JFLCC J-2 staff is detailed in Figure F-3. The following intelligence-related actions are the responsibility of the J-2 staff:

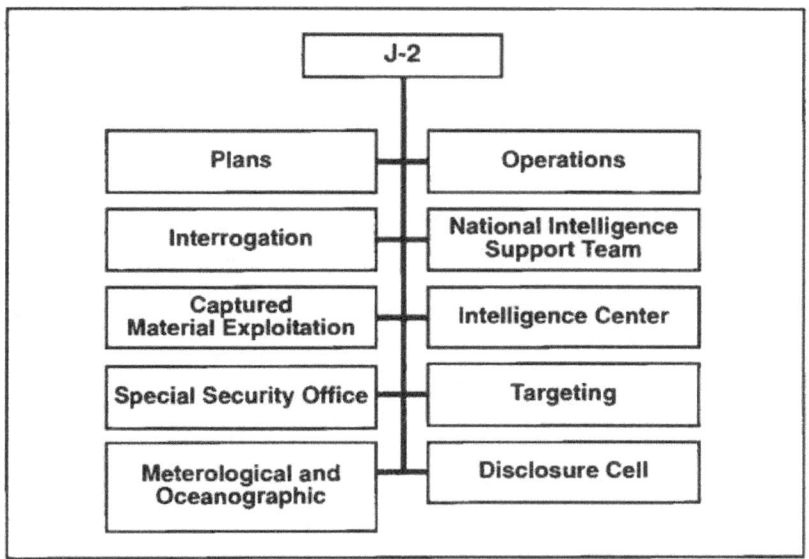

Figure F-3. Notional JFLCC J-2 Staff Section

- Maintain an intelligence watch in the operations and intelligence (O&I) center.

- Coordinate and maintain technical control over specialty, multi-disciplined intelligence and CI support to the commander and subordinate elements.

- Establish an all-source intelligence cell in, or adjacent to, the O&I center. The all-source cell is supported, as required, by coalition intelligence assets (if available) that remain under national control.

- Complete an initial intelligence estimate and maintain updates as required by the operational situation.

- Establish and maintain an intelligence collection management and RFI management system.

- Complete coalition all-source analysis and dissemination.

- Establish and maintain adversary and hostile databases to support operations and planning.

- Act as central point of contact for RFIs from subordinate staffs.

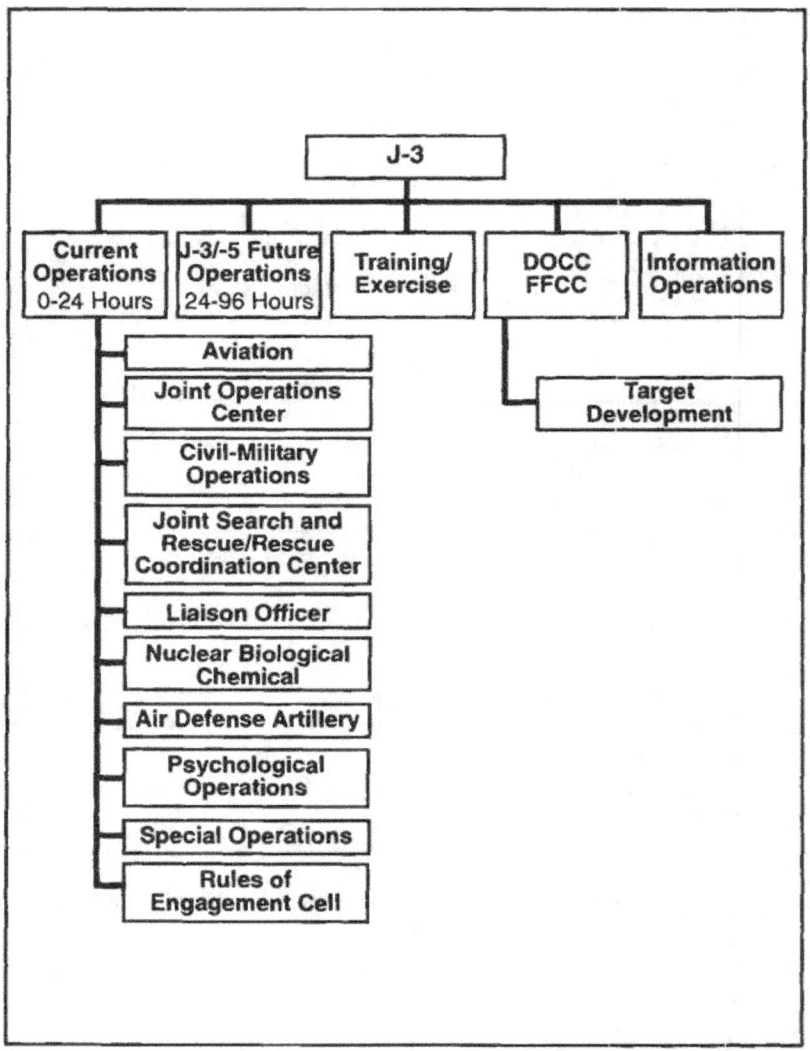

Figure F-4. Notional JFLCC J-3 Staff Section

F-8. The JFLCC J-4 formulates and implements logistics plans within the AO for forces assigned or attached to the land force. The JFLCC J-4 oversees the implementation of these plans by monitoring the logistics requirements of the JFLCC components and performs an analysis for logistical impacts on land operations. A notional JFLCC J-4 staff organization is depicted in Figure F-5. The following actions are the responsibility of the J-4:

- Monitors and coordinates the logistics functions and requirements of the JFLCC.
- Advises JFLCC concerning logistics matters affecting joint, combined, and coalition support to land operations.
- Prepares and/or assists the Service component G-4s on the concept of logistics support for the AO and the logistics annexes of JFLCC OPLANs and OPORDs.
- Recommends to JFLCC, within the guidelines established by the JFC, priorities for the allocation of logistics resources among assigned forces within the AO.
- Participates in joint/multinational logistics boards and centers that directly impact on land operations.
- Maintains liaison with the other JFLCC staff, agencies, and JFC counterparts to keep abreast of the current logistics, operational, and intelligence situations.

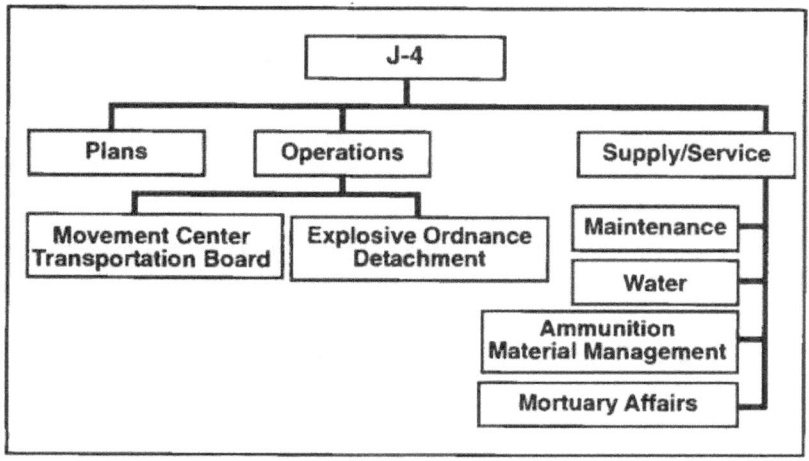

Figure F-5. Notional J-4 Staff Section

F-9. JFLCC J-5 operational planning addresses activities required for conducting land force operations. A notional JFLCC J-5 staff is depicted at Figure F-6. J-5 responsibilities for the employment and sustainment of land forces include:

- Employment planning prescribing how to apply force/forces to attain specified military objectives.
- Sustainment planning directed toward providing and maintaining levels of personnel, materiel, and consumables required to sustain the planned levels of combat activity for the estimated duration and at the desired level of intensity.

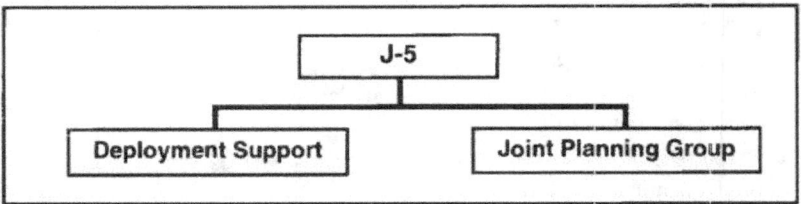

Figure F-6. Notional J-5 Staff Section

F-10. The J-6 staff provides theaterwide voice, data, and message connectivity between all components and MSCs/major subordinate elements. A notional J-6 staff organization is at Figure F-7. The following actions are the responsibility of the J-6:

- Advises the JFLCC and staff on all C^4 matters.
- Maintains overview of operations that require recommending changes in action or operations, as required.
- Oversees the establishment of a systems control (SYSCON) center to support top-level network control and management within the operations area and give direction and mission guidance.
- Prepares and reviews C^4 plans, policies, annexes, and operating instructions, as required, for JFLCC operations.
- Requests the necessary communications support resources through the JFC J-6. Identifies C^4 shortfalls to JFC J-6 for sourcing. Tasks subordinate components for C^4 support as required.
- Plans, coordinates, and activates, when required, C^4 facilities to provide rapid and reliable communications in support of the JFLCC.

- Submits request for intertheater communications security package use to the JFC and issues communications security (COMSEC) call-out message.
- Validates, consolidates, prioritizes, and forwards ultra-high frequency tactical satellite requirements to the JFC for channel allocation.
- Establishes, supervises, and revises, as necessary, the communications operating procedures pertaining to the unique JFLCC communications facilities.
- Conducts COMSEC management for JFLCC.
- Ensures that sound COMSEC principles are adhered to and ensures in-place availability of essential operation codes, authentication systems, and keying materials.
- Receives, reviews, and advises the JFLCC of COMSEC monitoring reports provided by COMSEC monitoring teams.
- Develops unique JFLCC signal operating instructions requirements and provides to JFC for review/coordination prior to dissemination.
- Consolidates and validates radio frequency requirements from components/warfighting elements and coordinates requests with the JFC.
- Provides guidance and assistance to supporting and assigned forces on all telecommunications and data systems matters for which JFLCC J-6 has jurisdiction.
- Consolidates and validates unique JFLCC telecommunications service requirements from components and coordinates with the appropriate agencies.
- Directs and conducts exercise/contingency planning.
- Determines user communications requirements.
- Develops critical circuit lists.
- Develops prioritized listing of systems/circuits for initial activation and provides to the SYSCON center for activation management.
- Develops prioritized listing of systems/circuits for deactivation and provides to the SYSCON center for management.
- Maintains understanding of future planning direction.
- Coordinates commercial satellite rights for military systems.

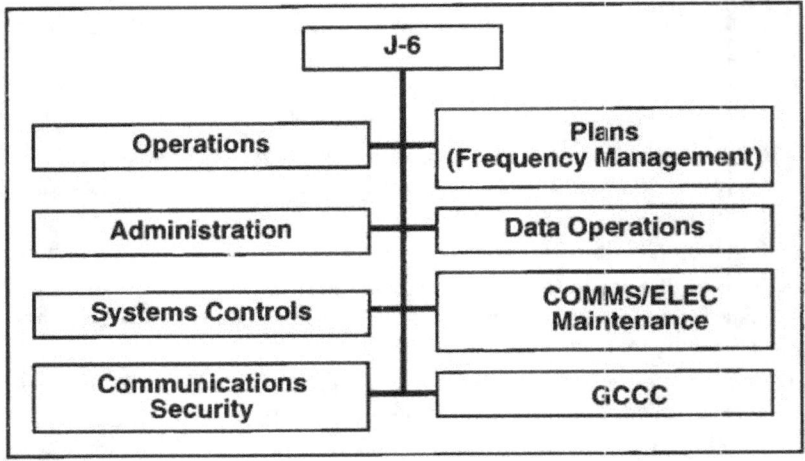

Figure F-7. Notional J-6 Staff Section

Appendix G

Multinational Considerations

GENERAL

G-1. To most effectively exploit the capabilities of multinational land forces, the multinational force commander (MNFC) normally designates an overall land component commander (LCC). The LCC must shift focus, tailor forces, and move from one role or mission to another rapidly and efficiently. In the absence of an LCC, the MNFC must plan, direct, and control land operations. Due to the complexity and fluidity of land operations, designation of an LCC may provide the MNFC greater flexibility to conduct multinational operations. Multinational force considerations consist of coalition and alliance operations. Each coalition or alliance will create the structure that best meets the needs, political goals, constraints, and objectives of the participating nations.

G-2. In alliance operations, such as those conducted by NATO, there are normally existing land commands that serve as the JFLCC or coalition force land component command.

G-3. In coalition operations, which are *ad hoc*, the JFC/coalition force commander (CFC) has the option to establish a land component command. When the JFC/CFC establishes a land component command, then the LCC and his staff must be aware of a myriad of additional issues that the JFLCC does not deal with because of the nature of coalition warfare. These issues include but are not limited to—

- C^2 considerations.
- Intelligence sharing.
- Operational constraints.
- ROEs.
- Logistics.

G-4. To be successful in coalition operations, it is imperative that sound and effective command relationships are developed. The national authorities providing forces to the coalition normally assign national forces under

OPCON/TACON of the CFC. The assignment of these national forces under OPCON/TACON may be qualified by caveats from the respective nations in accordance with their national policies. Further assignment to functional component commanders in an OPCON/TACON status by the CFC is subject to approval by the respective NCA.

LAND COMPONENT COMMAND HEADQUARTERS AND STAFF

G-5. The establishment of the land component command headquarters will most likely be based on the structure of the JFC headquarters. It may be a lead or framework nation headquarters, a parallel command structure, or both depending on the command structure of the coalition itself. In the lead or framework nation concept, appropriate C^2, communications, and intelligence procedures are determined by the lead or framework nation, working in close consultation with the other national contingents. In coalition operations, unity of effort must be achieved. The principle of unity of command also applies, but this principle may be more difficult to attain.

G-6. Depending on the size, complexity, and duration of the operation, staff augmentation from other national contingents may be required to supplement the lead nation LCC staff to ensure that the lead nation headquarters is representative of the entire coalition. Such augmentation may include designated deputies or assistant commanders, planners, and logisticians. This facilitates the planning process by providing the LCC with a source of expertise on coalition members. Augmentation is required if a coalition partner possesses unique organizations or capabilities not found in the forces of the lead nation.

G-7. The LCC staff should be composed of appropriate members in key positions from each country having forces in the coalition. Positions on the staff should be divided so that country representation and influence generally reflect the composition of the force, but are also based in part on the mission and type of operations to be conducted. Coalition commanders must also look at force composition as it applies to capabilities, limitations, and required support. The importance of knowing, trusting, and quickly reaching a comfort level with staff members may make it desirable for the LCC to handpick some members of his staff, such as the chief of staff or G-3.

COMMAND FOCUS

G-8. Successful coalitions are built on the commander's focus on the political objective, assigned mission, sensitivity to the needs of other coalition members, a willingness to compromise or come to a consensus when necessary, and mutual confidence.

G-9. The intangible considerations that guide the actions of all participants, especially the senior commander, are rapport, respect, knowledge of partners, team building, and patience. These factors cannot guarantee success for the coalition, but ignoring them can usually guarantee failure of the coalition in accomplishing its mission.

COORDINATION AND CONTROL

G-10. There are two essential structural enhancements that improve control of coalition forces: the establishment of a liaison network and coordination centers. Regardless of the command structure established, the need for effective liaison is vital in any coalition force.

G-11. The use of liaison is an invaluable confidence-building tool between the coalition force and subordinate commands. It also fosters a better understanding of mission and tactics, facilitates the transfer of vital information, enhances mutual trust, and develops an increased level of teamwork. It is also a significant source of information for the LCC about subordinate force readiness, training, and other factors. Early establishment reduces the fog and friction caused by incompatible communications systems, doctrine, and operating procedures. Once established, the liaison teams are the direct representatives of their respective commanders.

G-12. Another proven means of enhancing stability, synchronization, deconfliction, and interaction and improving control within a coalition is the use of a coordination center. Coalition forces should routinely create such a center in the early stages of any coalition effort, especially one that is operating under a parallel command structure. The coordination center can be used for C^2, and variations can organize and control a variety of functional areas, including logistics and civil-military operations. Initially, a coordination center can be the focal point for support issues such as force sustainment, medical support, infrastructure engineering, host-nation support, and movement control. However, as a coalition matures, the role of the coordination center can be expanded to include command activities. When a coordination center is activated, member nations provide action officers who are familiar with its activities. Coalition nations should be encouraged to augment this staff with linguists and requisite communications capabilities to maintain contact with their parent headquarters. Early establishment and staffing of skilled personnel adds to the success of such centers.

STANDARDIZE PROCEDURES

G-13. All coalition force troops must fully understand the mission, goals, and objectives of the operation. SOPs should be established.

G-14. SOPs should be clear and easy to understand. When there is a lead nation, its SOP is used for most purposes. The coalition force must remember that many countries are not staffed or equipped to offer a full spectrum of support. They may not possess a full array of combat support or combat service support assets, maps of the projected AO, or the capability to obtain or use intelligence and imagery data of the type commonly used by other coalition forces. These military forces probably will look to other nations for equipment and supplies. It is important to know what agreements exist with these forces before their arrival in the projected AO.

INTELLIGENCE COLLECTION AND DISSEMINATION

G-15. As every coalition is different, so too are the ways in which intelligence is collected and disseminated within the coalition. LCCs may use existing international standardization agreements to establish rules and policies or may tailor rules and policy based on theater guidance and national policy as contained in National Disclosure Policy 1. The following general principles provide a starting point:

- Maintain unity of effort.
- Make adjustments.
- Plan early and plan concurrently.
- Share all necessary information.
- Conduct complementary operations.

G-16. Classification may present a problem in releasing information, but keeping as much unclassified as feasible improves interoperability and trust within the coalition. The commander must know what his own and other nation's positions are on intelligence sharing. Early sharing of information during planning ensures that coalition requirements are clearly stated, that guidance supports the commander's intent, and the coalition uses procedures supportable by other nations.

G-17. An intelligence operational architecture must be established. A land component command intelligence center is necessary for merging and prioritizing the intelligence requirements. A standardized methodology for disseminating and exchanging intelligence is required as well as the exchange of intelligence liaison personnel. In some situations, there may be more than one level of intelligence required.

COMMUNICATIONS

G-18. The capability to communicate is fundamental to successful operations. Key to successful communications is the preparation during planning. The mission analysis and assessment process provides the opportunity for the land component command communications officer to identify communication requirements and evaluate in-country capability. Many communication issues can be resolved through equipment exchange and liaison teams. Continual liaison between communications planners helps alleviate interoperability issues.

G-19. Communication requirements vary with the mission, composition, and geography of the land component command AO. Interoperability is often constrained by the least technologically advanced nation. The land component command force should address the need for integrated communications among all forces early in the planning phase of the operation. Communications should be provided between the land component command and its coalition land subordinates, which may go through national contingent headquarters. In MOOTW, it is important to communicate with civilian agencies. In the transition phase/planning, the communications transition may involve follow-on units, commercial communications, or agencies like the United Nations being considered early in the operation

G-20. The LCC should plan for adequate communications to include the ability to communicate using voice (secure and nonsecure), data, and video teleconferencing. The LCC needs a deployable communications capability and enough trained operators for sustained operations, with multiple means of communication to avoid the possibility of a single-point failure.

INTEGRATION OF CAPABILITIES

G-21. Each participating nation provides its own distinct forces and capabilities to a coalition. These capabilities differ based on national interests, objectives, arms control limitations, doctrine, organization, training, leader development, and equipment, history, defense budget, and domestic politics. The orchestration of these capabilities into land component command operations is dependent on differences in organization, capabilities, and doctrine. If other nations are also involved, these differences will be much greater. Understanding these differences is the difference between success and failure in coalition operations. Units of the same type in one nation's army may not perform the same functions as units in another army. An engineer unit in one army may have capabilities to build roads or buildings, while another may be limited to laying out minefields or building defensive positions.

G-22. The LCC must integrate these capabilities to achieve the desired end state. Selecting the right mix is a challenge. The coalition staff must be proactive in understanding the capabilities and limitations of the nations in the coalition force. Representatives of each nation must be present during planning. If a unit is given a mission it is incapable of performing, the plan will not work. National representatives can ensure that taskings are appropriate to the force. If possible, national representatives should be available in each staff element. They must be thoroughly familiar with their nation's capabilities and limitations.

RULES OF ENGAGEMENT

G-23. ROEs are directives to military forces and individuals that define the circumstances, conditions, degree, and manner in which forces or actions may or may not be applied. Although the participants may have similar political mandates, each nation is likely to come to the coalition with different national ROEs reflecting its reason for entering the coalition. Some national ROEs are relatively free of constraint while others may be severely constrained. In many cases, commanders of deployed forces may lack the authority to speak on behalf of their nation in the ROE development process. Complete consensus or standardization of ROEs should be sought, but may not be achievable.

G-24. The LCC needs to reconcile differences as much as possible to develop and implement simple ROEs that can be tailored by member forces to their national policies. For the individual soldier to understand and implement ROEs, they must be clear and simple. Trying to obtain concurrence for ROEs from national authorities is a time-consuming process and should be addressed early in the planning process.

G-25. When consensus on ROEs cannot be achieved, the commander must consider how to employ multinational forces within their own ROEs.

LOGISTICS

G-26. Logistics are more complex in multinational operations and require more planning and coordination than that of a single nation. Although logistics is the overall responsibility of each contributing nation, some force-contributing nations do not have the assets to provide and/or transport their own logistical support when deployed and therefore must rely on nations with these capabilities. In these cases, the LCC must coordinate required support to both military and civilian organizations within the guidelines and plans of the higher level multinational command. Support may include both deployment and sustainment. For deployment, close liaison with theater airlift C^2 can assist in coordinating approval and facilitating airlift once approved. When support is required, ensure funding lines are clearly identified.

G-27. Unity of effort is essential to land component command logistics operations; however, multinational logistics planning is primarily the responsibility of the lead C-4, not land component command C-4. This requires coordination not only between nations, but also with civilian agencies in the AO. The execution of land component command logistics may be a collective responsibility, but must be coordinated and planned within the higher level multinational command guidance. When possible, mutual land-operations-oriented logistics support should be developed for economy of effort. Land component command logistics should be flexible, responsive, predictive, and provide timely sustainment throughout the entire force. The land component command logistics plan should incorporate the logistics requirements and capabilities of all land forces to ensure sustained and synchronized execution. Consensus on land component command logistics issues and requirements should be formed early. This requires thorough knowledge of coalition force doctrine and good relations with subordinate commanders and civilian leaders as well as cooperation and continuous coordination between all elements providing logistics support and the operational elements. This must begin during the initial planning phase and continue through the operation's termination. (Refer to JP 4-08 for further discussion.)

G-28. It is essential that logistics be planned for the entire coalition force with a single command providing as much control as possible and within the limitations of interoperability. The creation of a single coalition logistics command provides economy of assets and system efficiency. Even if coalition participants insist upon maintaining a national logistics structure, assigning a lead for logistics responsibility precludes duplication of effort. The G-4/S-4 should establish a planning group to define the extent of interoperability that exists between coalition forces. Funding authority to support coalition forces should be identified as early as possible and procedures developed to ensure there is no adverse impact on operations.

Operational Tasks

GENERAL

H-1. This appendix defines the role and responsibilities of the JFLCC by providing a menu of capabilities with associated conditions and standards that may be selected by the JFC to accomplish the mission. These tasks, derived from the UJTL, describe in broad terms the capabilities of our Armed Forces. The tasks described provide a common language (method) for stating capabilities required in the execution of joint/multinational operations.

SCOPE

H-2. The following three categories characterize the scope and level of JFLCC's involvement in performance of stated tasks, subordinate tasks, and enabling tasks generally at the operational level of war necessary for the land force to support/conduct campaigns and major operations.

- Responsibility. The JFLCC is actively and directly engaged in commanding, controlling, and directing the land force in accomplishment of tasks, subordinate tasks, and enabling tasks so designated.

- Influences. The JFLCC provides broad guidance sufficient to assure integration, synchronization, and full synergy of the efforts of each land force MSC, in the context of the overall ground operation, toward accomplishment of the tasks, subordinate tasks, and enabling tasks so designated. The JFLCC then monitors progress in execution of these, providing additional guidance only as required.

- Interest. The JFLCC requires some level of awareness and/or status on accomplishment of tasks, subordinate tasks, and enabling tasks so designated in order to effectively C^2 the ground forces but provides guidance only on an exception basis.

CORE TASKS/FUNCTIONS

H-1. The following is from a land force perspective. US land forces routinely have an organic aviation combat element whose operations are an integral and critical aspect of the land force's operations.

OP.1 OPERATIONAL MANEUVER
AND MOVEMENT
(JFLCC RESPONSIBILITY)

H-2. This is the disposition of joint and/or multinational land forces, conventional forces, and SOF to create a decisive impact on the conduct of a campaign or major operations by either securing the operational advantages of position before battle is joined or exploiting tactical success to achieve operational or strategic results. This activity includes moving or deploying land forces for operational advantage within a theater (or area) of operations and conducting maneuver to operational depths (for offensive or defensive purposes). It also includes enhancing the mobility of friendly forces, degrading the mobility of enemy forces, and controlling a land, sea, and air or space area for operational advantage. Movement and maneuver can be on the land, under the sea, or in the air. Operational formations are actually composed of groupings of tactical forces moving to achieve operational or strategic objectives.

OP.1.1 CONDUCT OPERATIONAL MOVEMENT
(JFLCC RESPONSIBILITY)

H-3. This is the regrouping, deploying, shifting, or moving of joint/multinational formations within a theater (or area) of operations from less threatening or less promising areas to more decisive positions elsewhere (that is, the friendly position obtained relative to the enemy) by any means (joint, allied, host nation, or third country) or mode (air, land, or sea).

OP.1.1.1 FORMULATE REQUEST FOR
STRATEGIC DEPLOYMENT OF JOINT/COMBINED
FORCES TO THEATER OF OPERATIONS
(JFLCC INFLUENCES)

H-4. The JFLCC recommends the land force operational plan. If this plan is approved by the JFLCC JFC, then the JFLCC's recommendations should influence the timing, sequence priority, and arrival location for land forces deploying into theater.

OP.1.1.2 CONDUCT INTRATHEATER OF OPERATIONS DEPLOYMENT OF FORCES (E.G., DEPLOYMENTS WITHIN THE THEATER [OR AREA] OF OPERATIONS) (JFLCC INFLUENCES)

H-5. The JFLCC recommends the land force plan. If this plan is approved, then the JFLCC's recommendations should influence the intratheater movement of forces in terms of allocating land, air, and, to some extent, maritime movement assets.

OP.1.2 CONDUCT OPERATIONAL MANEUVER (JFLCC RESPONSIBILITY)

H-6. This is the deployment of joint, multinational, operational, conventional, and SOF forces to and from battle formations and to extend forces to operational depths to achieve a position of advantage over the enemy for accomplishing operational or strategic objectives.

OP.1.2.1 TRANSITION TO AND FROM TACTICAL BATTLE FORMATIONS (JFLCC INFLUENCES)

H-7. The land force plan should indicate disposition of operational forces in terms of width and depth (land force battlefield geometry) to increase tactical readiness in conformance to the operational commander's campaign or major OPLAN and intent. JFLCC provides sufficient direction to ensure coordination of all land force activity, without meddling or overcontrol.

OP.1.2.2 POSTURE FORCES FOR OPERATIONAL FORMATIONS (JFLCC RESPONSIBILITY)

H-8. The land force plan should group forces and means into operational formations for the conduct of major operations and campaigns. Operational formations (e.g., echelons of combined arms organizations, like a MEF with Army maneuver and combat support, and combat service support forces) must support the commander's concept and provide for effective use of all forces, a capability for maneuvering and increasing the strength and means during the operation, a rapid transition from one type of operation to another without the loss of momentum or effectiveness, the conduct of continuous operations, and for protection of the force.

OP.1.2.3 CONDUCT OPERATIONS IN DEPTH
(JFLCC RESPONSIBILITY)

H-9. The JFLCC designs offensive and/or defensive land operations to operational depths to achieve a position of advantage (shapes the battlefield) for the defeat or neutralization of enemy operational forces. This may include amphibious, air, and space forces.

OP.1.3 PROVIDE OPERATIONAL MOBILITY
(JFLCC INFLUENCES)

H-10. Operational mobility facilitates the movement of joint and multinational operational formations in campaign or major operations without delays due to operationally significant terrain or obstacles.

OP.1.3.1 OVERCOME OPERATIONALLY SIGNIFICANT
OBSTACLES (JFLCC INFLUENCES)

H-11. To preserve freedom of movement by counteracting the effects of natural (existing/mountain ranges, depressions, sabkhas, major rivers, river deltas, marshlands, urban terrain, thick forests, etc.) and operationally significant obstacles (reinforcing/minefields, ditches, and other barriers), the JFLCC would assess then direct appropriate allocation of engineer mobility assets.

OP.1.3.2 ENHANCE MOVEMENT
OF OPERATIONAL FORCES
(JFLCC RESPONSIBILITY)

H-12. To prepare or improve facilities (e.g., airfields, landing zones, sea/river ports, transmodal transload areas) and routes (e.g., roads, railroads, canals, rivers) of travel for moving operational forces. This should also involve the JFLCC communicating expectations as far as the future use of these facilities. If future offensive operations rely on the use of the enemy's railway system, then the JFLCC provides guidance on what needs to be preserved for future use yet still denying the present use to the enemy.

OP.1.4 PROVIDE OPERATIONAL COUNTERMOBILITY
(JFLCC INFLUENCES)

H-13. To delay, channel, or stop offensive air, land, and sea movement by enemy operational formations to help create positional advantage for friendly joint and multinational operational forces and expose enemy COGs or high payoff targets to destruction.

OP.1.4.1 SELECT LOCATION FOR OPERATIONAL OBSTACLES (JFLCC RESPONSIBILITY)

H-14. Identify air, land, and sea sites for reinforcing or constructing obstacles to take maximum advantage of existing obstacles to form a system of obstacles (normally on a large scale) for operational effect, while providing flexibility of friendly movement and increasing the variety of obstacles the enemy must encounter (this would be integrated with the overall operational design). This implies that once the land force plan is developed, appropriate guidance in the form of designating obstacle zones and obstacle-free/restricted zones should be indicated (if appropriate) to ensure that subordinate tactical obstacle employment does not interfere with current or planned land force maneuver. (For example, the battle of Kursk involved an integrated defense by multiple corps and armies. This was accomplished not by simply coordinating the obstacle plans of subordinate formations but through operational design.)

OP.1.4.2 EMPLACE OPERATIONAL SYSTEMS OF OBSTACLES (JFLCC INFLUENCES)

H-15. Develop existing obstacle and reinforce terrain with countermobility means (e.g., minefields, demolition).

OP.1.5 CONTROL OPERATIONALLY SIGNIFICANT AREA (JFLCC RESPONSIBILITY)

H-16. The JFLCC should develop plans that dominate or control the physical environment whose possession provides either side an operational advantage, thus denying it to the enemy by either occupying the operationally key area or limiting enemy use or access to the environment or area. For an environment or area to be operationally key, its dominance or control must achieve operational or strategic results or deny same to the enemy. In MOOTW, control of operationally significant areas also pertains to assisting a friendly country in populace and resource control.

OP.2 OPERATIONAL FIREPOWER
(JFLCC RESPONSIBILITY)

H-17. The JFLCC's targeting guidance and recommendations concerning the application of operational fires through all available means and systems in support of land force operations will be a significant input in the effort to develop an integrated multi-dimensional/multi-medium attack of the enemy's COGs and shaping of the battlefield. The JFLCC is concerned with the application of firepower and nonlethal means to achieve a decisive operational impact (may be decisive in itself or may contribute to decisive results in synchronization with other operational means). Operational firepower (e.g., all types of ordnance, bombs, rockets, missiles, artillery) is by its nature primarily a joint/multinational activity or task.

OP.2.1 PROCESS OPERATIONAL TARGETS
(JFLCC INFLUENCES)

H-18. The JFLCC should provide targeting guidance which aids in positively identifying and selecting land targets of major/decisive impact and match appropriate joint and multinational operational firepower. This is based on operational design and intended impact which influences the type of target to be attacked and the efforts of intelligence forces to produce these targets. The term target is used in its broadest sense to include targets of all types including targets in MOOTW, such as a target audience of psychological operations (PSYOP) in a counterinsurgency situation.

OP.2.1.1 SELECT OPERATIONAL
TARGETS FOR ATTACK
(JFLCC INFLUENCES)

H-19. Evaluate each operational target to determine if and when it should be attacked for optimum effect on enemy COGs and operational commander's intent.

OP.2.1.2 ALLOCATE JOINT/MULTINATIONAL
OPERATIONAL FIRES RESOURCES
(JFLCC RESPONSIBILITY)

H-20. Apportion operational firepower resources for the priority employment of joint and multinational firepower systems on operational targets according to the commander's plans and intent. Basically, the JFLCC focuses and prioritizes the land component targeting effort and allocates the limited land component deep fires assets.

OP.2.2 ATTACK OPERATIONAL TARGETS
(JFLCC RESPONSIBILITY)

H-21. To enter into conflict with the enemy to destroy operational level targets (target sets) (targets which have operational impact) and to shape and control the tempo of campaigns using all available joint and multinational operational firepower assets (including naval, air, space, ground, long-range cannon, rockets and missile, SOF, conventional and special munitions, and PSYOP) against land targets having operational significance.

OP.2.2.1 CONDUCT LETHAL ATTACK FOR
OPERATIONAL TARGETS
(JFLCC INFLUENCES)

H-22. Engages operational land targets with available joint and multinational firepower delivery systems. To delay, disrupt, destroy, or degrade enemy operational forces in critical tasks and facilities (e.g., command, control, communications, and intelligence targets).

OP.2.2.1.1 CONDUCT ATTACK WITH
SURFACE/SUBSURFACE-BASED
OPERATIONAL FIREPOWER
(JFLCC INFLUENCES)

H-23. Employ surface and subsurface land- and sea-based joint and multinational operational fire to destroy, suppress, or neutralize enemy operational forces, fortifications, and critical tasks and facilities.

OP.2.2.1.2 CONDUCT ATTACK WITH
AEROSPACE OPERATIONAL FIREPOWER
(JFLCC INFLUENCES)

H-24. To engage joint/multinational air and/or space forces (including helicopters, unmanned aerial vehicle, space vehicles) operational fires to destroy, suppress, or neutralize enemy operational targets.

OP.2.2.2 CONDUCT NONLETHAL ATTACK ON OPERATIONAL TARGETS (JFLCC INFLUENCES)

H-25. Engages operational land targets with joint and multinational means designed to destroy, impair, disrupt, or delay the performance of enemy operational forces, tasks, and facilities. The means include PSYOP, SOF, EW (jamming), and other command and control warfare (C^2W). PSYOP propaganda and action are aimed at making the enemy believe he cannot win causing him to withdraw. PSYOP consolidation activities are planned activities in peacetime, MOOTW, and war directed at the civilian population located in areas under friendly control in order to achieve desired behavior which supports the military objectives and operational freedom of the supported commander. PSYOP activities support theater military strategic objectives and campaign or major operations objectives.

OP.2.2.2.1 DESTROY OR REDUCE ENEMY OPERATIONAL FORCE EFFECTIVENESS (JFLCC RESPONSIBILITY)

H-26. To create delays in enemy operational movement to disrupt enemy C^2, to degrade human and equipment performance, and to affect enemy force's will to fight. Means include PSYOP.

OP.2.2.2.2 DESTROY OR REDUCE ENEMY CRITICAL FACILITIES EFFECTIVENESS (JFLCC INFLUENCES)

H-27. To use SOF and nonlethal chemical and EW with the object of degrading, disrupting, or temporarily impairing critical tasks or facilities.

OP.2.3 INTEGRATE OPERATIONAL FIREPOWER (JFLCC RESPONSIBILITY)

H-28. To integrate operational firepower on single or multiple operational targets at the decisive time and place. Thus focusing and synchronizing the effort producing full synergy and maximum operational impact. This integration uses lethal and nonlethal attacks that include friendly C^2W and EW measures and minimizing their effect on friendly forces, neutrals, and noncombatants.

OP.3 OPERATIONAL PROTECTION
(JFLCC INFLUENCES)

H-29. The conservation of the fighting potential of a force so that it can be applied at the decisive time and place. The activity includes actions taken to counter enemy's firepower and maneuver by making service members, systems, and operational formations difficult to locate, strike, and destroy. Operational protection includes protecting joint and multinational land, sea, and aerospace forces; bases; and lines of communication (LOC) from enemy operational maneuver and concentrated enemy air, sea, and ground attack, natural occurrences, and terrorist attack. This task also pertains to protection of operational level forces, systems, and civil infrastructure of friendly nations and groups in MOOTW.

OP.3.1 PROVIDE OPERATIONAL
AEROSPACE DEFENSE
(JFLCC INFLUENCES)

H-30. The protection of operational forces from air attack (including attack from or through space) through both direct defense and destruction of the enemy's air attack capacity in the air is performed in conjunction with (ICW) the AADC. This task includes such measures as use of aircraft (includes helicopters), interceptor missiles, air defense artillery, weapons not used primarily in an air defense role, and electronic countermeasures.

OP.3.1.1 PROCESS OPERATIONAL
AEROSPACE TARGETS
(JFLCC INTEREST)

H-31. To select offensive air threats to the operational environment and attach appropriate response to ensure freedom of action for campaigns, major operations, and protection of key assets.

OP.3.1.1.1 ALLOCATE TARGETS FOR ATTACK
(JFLCC INTEREST)

H-32. To designate specific targets to operational air defense units (land, sea, and air [includes space]) for interception or engagement.

OP.3.1.1.2 INTEGRATE JOINT/COMBINED OPERATIONAL AEROSPACE DEFENSE (JFLCC INFLUENCES)

H-33. To achieve a balanced mix of all available joint and multinational operational air defense forces (aircraft, missiles, air defense artillery) of air, land, and naval components. This task is performed ICW the AADC.

OP.3.1.2 PROVIDE AEROSPACE CONTROL (JFLCC INFLUENCE)

H-34. To provide safe, efficient, and flexible use of airspace (includes space).

OP.3.1.2.1 EMPLOY POSITIVE CONTROL MEASURES (JFLCC INFLUENCES)

H-35. To establish direct controls that minimize mutual interference between operational air defense and other operations. This task is performed ICW the AADC.

OP.3.1.2.2 EMPLOY PROCEDURAL CONTROL MEASURES (JFLCC INTEREST)

H-36. To establish readily identifiable electronic, visual, or other means of identification critical to survival of friendly aircraft in the event positive control fails.

OP.3.1.3 ATTACK ENEMY AEROSPACE TARGETS (JFLCC INTEREST)

H-37. To intercept, engage, destroy, or neutralize enemy operational air formations (includes aircraft, missiles, and space vehicles) in flight using all available air defense capabilities of all friendly forces to achieve operational results. This task is performed ICW the AADC.

OP.3.1.3.1 CONDUCT LETHAL ATTACK
ON OPERATIONAL AEROSPACE TARGETS
(JFLCC INTEREST)

H-38. To employ air-to-air (includes space systems and armed helicopters), surface-to-air, and subsurface-to-air joint and multinational operational forces as early and as far forward as possible to protect friendly operational air, land, and sea forces by attacking enemy air defense targets in support of campaign plans, major operations, and forces in the COMMZ and operationally significant facilities in the combat zone. This task is performed ICW the AADC.

OP.3.1.3.2 CONDUCT NONLETHAL ATTACK
ON OPERATIONAL AEROSPACE TARGETS
(JFLCC INTEREST)

H-39. To employ supplementary means such as mass jamming and electronic support measures to deny, disrupt, and degrade enemy air attack sensors, guidance systems, and C^2 systems.

OP.3.2 PROVIDE PROTECTION
OF OPERATIONAL FORCES AND MEANS
(JFLCC INFLUENCES)

H-40. To safeguard friendly COGs and operational forces potential by reducing or avoiding the effects of enemy operational level, and unintentional, actions (to include movement and radio electronic combat). In MOOTW, this activity includes protection of governmental and civil infrastructure and populace of the country being supported; this includes AT.

OP.3.2.1 PREPARE OPERATIONALLY
SIGNIFICANT FORTIFICATIONS
(JFLCC INFLUENCES)

H-41. To provide protective construction hardening for operational forces and key facilities, (e.g., C^2, logistics, and rear area positions and fighting positions). This activity provides protection of governmental and civil infrastructure and the populace of the country being supported, including AT measures.

OP.3.2.2 REMOVE OPERATIONALLY SIGNIFICANT HAZARDS (JFLCC INFLUENCE)

H-42. To eliminate the presence of hazards which could adversely affect execution of the operational commander's plan.

OP.3.2.2.1 EMPLOY PSYOP IN THEATER OF OPERATIONS (JOA COMMANDER/JFLCC INTEREST)

H-43. To plan and execute operations to convey selected information and indicators to foreign audiences in theaters of operation/JOA to influence their emotions, motives, objective reasoning, and, ultimately, the behavior of foreign governments, organizations, groups, and individuals.

OP.3.2.3 PROTECT USE OF THE ELECTROMAGNETIC SPECTRUM (JFLCC INTEREST)

H-44. To take actions to ensure friendly effective use of the electromagnetic spectrum despite the enemy's use of EW. This is a division of EW and also called electronic counter-countermeasures.

OP.3.2.4 PROVIDE POSITIVE IDENTIFICATION OF FRIENDLY OPERATIONAL FORCES (JFLCC RESPONSIBILITY)

H-45. To discretely and positively determine by any means the individuality (friendly and enemy) of operational level forces, objects (such as air, space, land, or sea formations), or of phenomena (e.g., communications-electronic patterns). To distinguish these forces from hostile or unknown forces and means one from the other.

OP.3.3 EMPLOY OPERATIONS SECURITY (JFLCC INFLUENCES)

H-46. To take action to avoid friendly force indicators associated with planning and conducting campaigns and major operations from the enemy (includes terrorists) commander's perspective and thus protect intentions.

OP.3.3.1 EMPLOY SIGNAL SECURITY
(JFLCC INTEREST)

H-47. To protect emitters and information transmitted through friendly operational C^2 electronic systems from enemy exploitation.

OP.3.3.2 EMPLOY CONCEALMENT TECHNIQUES
(JFLCC INTEREST)

H-48. To provide protection of operational forces and facilities from enemy observation and surveillance sensors.

OP.3.3.3 AVOID OPERATIONAL PATTERNS
(JFLCC INFLUENCES)

H-49. To vary activities and ways of conducting operations to avoid predictable patterns which are vulnerable to enemy interception.

OP.3.4 CONDUCT DECEPTION
IN SUPPORT OF SUBORDINATE CAMPAIGNS
AND MAJOR OPERATIONS
(JFLCC RESPONSIBILITY)

H-50. To manipulate enemy operational commander's perceptions and expectations into a false picture of reality that conceals friendly actions and intentions until it is too late for enemy operational forces to react effectively within context of the theater commander's deception plan. Several measures are available to a commander for conducting deception, to include physical, technical, or electronic (imitative, manipulative, and simulative), and administration.

OP.3.4.1 PROTECT DETAILS
OF CAMPAIGN PLANS AND
MAJOR OPERATIONS
(JFLCC RESPONSIBILITY)

H-51. To take actions to prevent the enemy from learning the true intent of operational commander's campaign and major operational plans and deception plans. The activity includes limiting, to the last possible moment, the number of people aware of friendly plans; delaying or masking operational movements and preparations; deceiving friendly leaders and personnel where necessary; and other appropriate actions.

OP.3.4.2 SPREAD MISINFORMATION REGARDING CONDUCT OF CAMPAIGNS AND MAJOR OPERATIONS (JFLCC INFLUENCES)

H-52. To develop and disseminate the deception plan focused on enemy expectations, preconceptions, and fears concerning friendly intent in order to deceive the enemy operational commander of the true friendly intentions regarding campaigns and major operations. The deception plan will use the entire joint and multinational forces and strategic means, as appropriate, to deceive the enemy.

OP.3.4.3 ASSESS EFFECT OF OPERATIONAL DECEPTION PLAN (JFLCC RESPONSIBILITY)

H-53. To determine the extent to which the deception story and related actions have had on the plans and actions of the opposing operational commander and his staff.

OP.3.5 PROVIDE SECURITY FOR OPERATIONAL FORCES AND MEANS (JFLCC INFLUENCES)

H-54. To enhance the freedom of action by identifying and reducing friendly vulnerability to hostile acts, influence, or surprise. This includes measures to protect from surprise, observation, detection, interference, espionage, terrorists, and sabotage. This activity includes actions for protecting and securing flanks and rear area of operational formations and protecting and securing critical installations, facilities, and systems.

OP.4 OPERATIONAL COMMAND AND CONTROL (JFLCC RESPONSIBILITY)

H-55. The exercise of authority and direction by a properly designated commander over assigned and attached operational forces in the accomplishment of the mission. C^2 activities are performed through arrangement of personnel, equipment, communications, facilities, and procedures employed by an operational commander in planning, directing, coordinating, and controlling forces in conducting campaigns and major operations to accomplish the mission. This operating system is applicable across the range of military operations including MOOTW.

OP.4.1 ACQUIRE AND COMMUNICATE
OPERATIONAL LEVEL INFORMATION
AND MAINTAIN STATUS
(JFLCC RESPONSIBILITY)

H-56. To gain and possess information of the theater of operations military objective, enemy operational forces and COGs, friendly operational forces, terrain, and weather (includes characteristics of AO, climate) by or for the operational commander or his staff. To translate that information into usable form and to retain and disseminate it. This activity includes informing and advising the theater-of-war commander and securing an understanding of strategic guidance or an understanding of national and alliance policy, objectives, and strategic aim, other elements of national and multinational power (e.g., political, economic, informational), and theater strategic objectives. At the operational level, this task includes interfacing with friendly and enemy (in occupied territory) civilian government authorities in the operational commander's area of responsibility. This activity includes dissemination of any type information.

OP.4.1.1 COMMUNICATE
OPERATIONAL INFORMATION
(JFLCC RESPONSIBILITY)

H-57. To send and receive operationally significant data from one echelon of command to another by any means.

OP.4.1.2 MANAGE MEANS
OF COMMUNICATING
OPERATIONAL INFORMATION
(JFLCC RESPONSIBILITY)

H-58. To direct, establish, or control the means used in sending or receiving operational information of any kind and to use communication networks and modes for obtaining or sending operational information. C^2 systems include systems required for support to other agencies of the US Government, friendly nations, and groups in MOOTW.

OP.4.1.3 MAINTAIN OPERATIONAL INFORMATION AND FORCE STATUS (JFLCC RESPONSIBILITY)

H-59. To screen, circulate, store, and display operational data in a form suitable for the decision-making process of the operational commander and his staff and for supporting other US governmental agencies, friendly nations, and groups in the region.

OP.4.1.4 MONITOR STRATEGIC SITUATION (JFLCC RESPONSIBILITY)

H-60. To be aware of and to understand national and alliance objective, policies, goals, other elements of national and alliance power (political, economic, informational), political aim, and the theater-of-war commander's strategic concept and intent.

OP.4.2 ASSESS OPERATIONAL SITUATION (JFLCC RESPONSIBILITY)

H-61. To continuously evaluate information received through reports or the personal observations of the commander on the general situation in the theater (or area) of operation and conduct of the campaign or major operation. In particular, this activity includes deciding whether different actions are required from those that would result from the most recent orders issued. This includes evaluating operational requirements in terms of doctrine, training, leader development, organizations, materiel, and concepts.

OP.4.2.1 REVIEW CURRENT SITUATION (JFLCC RESPONSIBILITY)

H-62. To examine on-hand operational information. This includes analyzing the assigned mission (includes assigned strategic military and politico-military objectives) and related tasks in the context of the next higher echelon's campaign plan or OPORD, the strategic aim, and the combining of on-hand with incoming information while separating critical from noncritical information.

OP.4.2.2 PROJECT FUTURE CAMPAIGNS OR MAJOR OPERATIONS (JFLCC RESPONSIBILITY)

H-63. To see beyond immediate battles and estimate enemy's future actions and to anticipate friendly actions for employment of operational forces after each phase of a current campaign or major operation (sequels), to include consideration of possible local reversals or tactical failures.

OP.4.2.3 DECIDE ON NEED FOR ACTION OR CHANGE (JFLCC RESPONSIBILITY)

H-64. To decide whether actions are required which are different from those which operational forces (or supported friendly governments) have already been directed (or decided) to execute.

OP.4.3 DETERMINE OPERATIONAL ACTIONS (JFLCC RESPONSIBILITY)

H-65. To conduct the process of making detailed staff estimates and decisions for implementing the theater commander's theater strategy and campaign plans, associated sequels, and anticipated campaigns or major operations. This activity includes determining solutions to operational level needs.

OP.4.3.1 ISSUE PLANNING GUIDANCE (JFLCC RESPONSIBILITY)

H-66. To establish guidance for planning tasks to be accomplished by subordinate commands and the operational commander's staff. This includes initial and subsequent planning guidance. Planning guidance would include constraints and restrictions such as ROEs for firepower, maneuver, air defense, and so forth.

OP.4.3.2 DEVELOP COURSES OF ACTION (JFLCC RESPONSIBILITY)

H-67. To anticipate and define multiple, feasible employment options within the framework of the next senior commander's concept.

OP.4.3.3 ANALYZE COURSES OF ACTION
(JFLCC RESPONSIBILITY)

H-68. To examine and wargame each COA to determine its advantages and disadvantages. Each friendly COA is wargamed against each enemy COA.

OP.4.3.4 COMPARE COURSES OF ACTION
(JFLCC RESPONSIBILITY)

H-69. To analyze the various COAs against each other by either comparing its advantages and disadvantages of each COA previously analyzed or to isolate and compare decisive significant factors that are selected based on each situation.

OP.4.3.5 SELECT OR MODIFY
COURSES OF ACTION
(JFLCC RESPONSIBILITY)

H-70. To decide on the COA which offers the best prospect for success. This also includes modifying a COA previously selected and is therefore a continuous process.

OP.4.3.6 FINALIZE COMMANDER'S CONCEPT
AND INTENT
(JFLCC RESPONSIBILITY)

H-71. To restate the mission (includes assigned strategic military objectives), develop the CONOPS (operational movement and firepower), give clear statement of commander's initial intent (aim of entire campaign or major operation), and derive subordinates' tasks and objectives. This task pertains to air, land, and sea forces and those of a supported US governmental agency or nation in MOOTW (that is the supported organization's concept and intent). The CONOPS could include: allocation of forces, phasing, means of reinforcing maneuver, firepower, combat air force requirements, priorities by phase, maritime support, use of combat area (and subordinates and supporting commands such as space systems), SOF employment, special weapons employment, and deception. Special types of operations, for example, amphibious, may include other elements. This task could include a restatement of ROEs and other restrictions and constraints.

OP.4.4 DIRECT AND LEAD SUBORDINATE OPERATIONAL FORCES (JFLCC RESPONSIBILITY)

H-72. To establish command climate which provides direction to subordinates, and supporting commands, such that they understand their mission and military objectives and their contribution to attainment of the commander's concept and intent and assigned strategic military objectives including those of a supported commander. This includes maximum decentralized conduct of campaigns and major operations, either detailed or mission-type plans and orders as time and situation permit, maximum use of concurrent planning and coordination of plans and order with subordinate/higher headquarters, latitude for subordinate innovative risk-taking, and exploitation of opportunities or deliberate contemplative action as the theater and national situation dictate.

OP.4.4.1 PREPARE CAMPAIGN OR MAJOR OPERATIONS RELATED PLANS AND ORDERS (JFLCC RESPONSIBILITY)

H-73. To develop a plan or order which executes the concept and intent of the theater-of-war commander's campaign plan or that of a supported commander. Plans include intelligence collection of essential elements of information, logistic plans, ROEs, and so forth.

OP.4.4.1.1 DEVELOP AND COMPLETE OPERATIONAL PLANS AND ORDERS (JFLCC RESPONSIBILITY)

H-74. To finalize orders or plans prior to approval and issuance.

OP.4.4.1.2 COORDINATE SERVICE COMPONENT, THEATER, AND OTHER SUPPORT (JFLCC INFLUENCES)

H-75. To coordinate with allies, service component commands, theater commander, and adjacent, subordinate, higher, and supporting organizations to ensure cooperation and mutual support, a consistent effort, and a mutual understanding of the operational commander's priorities, support requirements, concept and intent, and objectives. This task includes coordination with ambassadors, country teams (as appropriate), and leaders of supported nations and other US agencies throughout the range of operations. This activity includes but is not limited to concept, sustainment support, and supporting component OPLANs. Coordination of air, land, and sea support begins early in the process.

OP.4.4.1.3 APPROVE PLANS AND ORDERS
(JFLCC RESPONSIBILITY)

H-76. To obtain the operational commander's approval and the next higher commander's approval of fully rationalized joint/multinational plans and orders prior to issuance.

OP.4.4.2 ISSUE PLANS AND ORDERS
(JFLCC RESPONSIBILITY)

H-77. To submit orders, plans, and reports for transmission to subordinate, supporting, or attached units for execution and to adjacent and higher units for coordination. The transmission of orders and plans by any means is part of the activity.

OP.4.4.3 PROVIDE OPERATIONAL
COMMAND PRESENCE
(JFLCC RESPONSIBILITY)

H-78. To position the operational commander so as to infuse among subordinates his will and intent or otherwise achieve the operational or strategic objectives of the campaign or operation.

OP.4.4.4 SYNCHRONIZE OPERATIONS
(JFLCC RESPONSIBILITY)

H-79. To arrange land, sea, and air operational forces in time, space, and purpose to produce maximum relative combat power at the decisive point. This activity includes the vertical and the horizontal integration of tasks in time and space to maximize combat output. Synchronization is the activity that ensures that all elements of the operational force, including supported agencies' and nations' forces, are efficiently and safely employed to maximize the sum of their effects beyond the sum of their individual capabilities. This includes synchronizing support to the supported commander.

OP.4.5 EMPLOY
COMMAND AND CONTROL WARFARE
(JFLCC RESPONSIBILITY)

H-80. To integrate the use of OPSEC, military deception, jamming, and physical destruction, supported by intelligence, to deny information, to influence, degrade, or destroy adversary C^2 capabilities and to protect friendly C^2 against such actions.

OP.5 DEVELOP
OPERATIONAL INTELLIGENCE
(JFLCC RESPONSIBILITY)

H-81. That intelligence which is required for the planning and conduct of subordinate campaigns and major operations within a theater (or area) of operation. At the operational level of war, the joint and multinational intelligence system concentrates on the collection of information, and the analysis of that information, which leads to the identification and location of the operational COGs (or high-payoff targets affecting the COGs) that, if successfully attacked, will achieve the assigned strategic aims.

OP.5.1 DEVELOP
OPERATIONAL INTELLIGENCE REQUIREMENTS
(JFLCC RESPONSIBILITY)

H-82. To determine and rank order intelligence requirements for the collection and processing of information in developing operational intelligence. In MOOTW, this activity also pertains to support of host nations or groups in determining their operational intelligence requirements. This includes monitoring availability of collected data and planning manpower and intelligence architecture needs.

OP.5.2 COLLECT OPERATIONAL INFORMATION
(JFLCC RESPONSIBILITY)

H-83. To gather information from US and allied operational, strategic, and tactical sources relative to threat operational forces and their COGs (and related high-payoff targets) and to the nature and characteristics of the assigned AOs (includes AOI). Operational level surveillance and reconnaissance are pertinent throughout this task.

OP.5.2.1 COLLECT INFORMATION ON ENEMY OPERATIONAL SITUATION AND HAZARDS (JFLCC INFLUENCES)

H-84. To obtain information on enemy (and friendly) operational force vulnerabilities, threat operational doctrine and forces (land, sea, and air) dispositions and order of battle, and the nature and characteristics of the AOs, to include significant hazards, such as NBC contamination of large areas. This activity includes collecting counterintelligence information.

OP.5.2.2 COLLECT INFORMATION ON OPERATIONAL TARGETS (JFLCC INFLUENCES)

H-85. To obtain information that supports the detection, identification, and location of enemy strategic and operational COGs and high-payoff targets whose attack will lead directly or indirectly to the defeat of the enemy. Distinguishing enemy target information from friendly forces and assessing damage to operational targets is included under this task.

OP.5.3 PROCESS OPERATIONAL INFORMATION (JFLCC RESPONSIBILITY)

H-86. To convert operational information into intelligence through collation, evaluation, analysis, integration, and interpretation. This activity includes the evaluation of threat joint and multinational operational land, sea, and air forces; insurgents or counterinsurgents, terrorists, and narcotics traffickers; the nature and characteristics of the theater (or area) of operations, to include the operational commander's AOI; and integration of threat information to determine operational and strategic COGs and assessing the enemy's C^2W capabilities, actions, and vulnerabilities.

OP.5.3.1 EVALUATE OPERATIONAL THREAT INFORMATION (JFLCC RESPONSIBILITY)

H-87. To continuously analyze the enemy in terms of his mobilization potential; military-strategic and operational organization (including alliance forces); and dispositions, doctrine, capabilities, C^2 structure, and decision-making processes. To evaluate enemy (and friendly) vulnerabilities. This evaluation includes continuous refinement of the order of battle for the entire array of the joint and multinational forces available to the enemy operational commander, personalities, and history of performance, the doctrine for employment of operational forces, and threat associated with MOOTW. Assessment of enemy C^2W capabilities is included here.

OP.5.3.2 ANALYZE AREA OF OPERATIONS
(JFLCC RESPONSIBILITY)

H-88. To conduct an analysis of the nature and characteristics of the theater (or area) of operations to determine the types and scale of operations area, the impact of significant regional features, and hazards on the conduct of both friendly and enemy campaigns or major operations. The analysis includes the impact of strategic limiting factors (such as ROEs) and determination of the operational commander's AOI. Significant regional features include political, economic, industrial, geographic, demographic, topographic, hydrographic, climatic (for example, weather, terrain), populace, cultural, lingual, historical, and psychological features of the area. This activity also includes analysis of significant alterations to the AOs that create operationally significant hazards (such as NBC contamination of large areas).

OP.5.3.3 INTEGRATE
OPERATIONAL INTELLIGENCE
(JFLCC RESPONSIBILITY)

H-89. To develop operational level, time-phased intelligence by combining data from the evaluation of the nature and characteristics of the area and the analysis of the threat to yield the enemy commander's intentions, COGs, and high-payoff targets.

OP.5.3.3.1 DEVELOP
ENEMY OPERATIONAL INTENTIONS
(JFLCC RESPONSIBILITY)

H-90. To form patterns from significant events, enemy national and alliance issues, or enemy operational commander's style which signal probable enemy operational intentions and probable COAs, thus revealing high-payoff targets or COGs for attack. This task includes identification of friendly vulnerabilities.

OP.5.3.3.2 DEVELOP
ENEMY OPERATIONAL TARGET INFORMATION
(JFLCC RESPONSIBILITY)

H-91. To provide timely and accurate locations of enemy operational forces that will impact current and future campaigns and major operations. Target data is derived from national, joint, and multinational sources and identifies high-payoff targets that, if attacked, will lead to the defeat of enemy COGs. This target information development includes enemy C^2W targets.

OP.5.3.3.3 IDENTIFY ENEMY VULNERABILITIES
(JFLCC RESPONSIBILITY)

H-92. To identify, for exploitation, patterns of significant events and activities, military and political issues, alliance relationships, and campaign styles of adversary operational commanders. These vulnerabilities include forces to be targeted for C^2W, EW, deception operations, and security weaknesses.

OP.5.3.4 DEVELOP INDICATIONS AND WARNING
(JFLCC RESPONSIBILITY)

H-93. To determine changes in the military, political, economic, social, and diplomatic behavior of the enemy that could lead to hostile activity to preclude strategic surprise.

OP.5.3.5 DEVELOP INTELLIGENCE COLLECTION PLANS
(JFLCC RESPONSIBILITY)

H-94. To determine gaps in intelligence and address essential elements of information in a plan for collecting the intelligence. The intent of the effort is to focus on key decisions and defeat mechanisms.

OP.5.4 PREPARE AND DISSEMINATE
OPERATIONAL INTELLIGENCE REPORTS
(JFLCC RESPONSIBILITY)

H-95. To formulate and convey operational intelligence estimates, annexes, and reports on the threat operational situation, intentions, vulnerabilities, targets (to include high-payoff targets and enemy COGs), characteristics of the theater of operations/AO, and other appropriate intelligence reports.

OP.6 PROVIDE
OPERATIONAL SUPPORT
(JFLCC INTEREST)

H-96. Those logistical and other support activities required to sustain the force in campaigns and major operations within a theater (or area) of operations. Operational sustainment extends from the theater-of-operations sustaining base (COMMZ) or bases, or forward sustaining bases in a smaller theater, to the forward combat service support units, resources, and facilities organic to major tactical organizations. This theater-of-operations sustaining base, in performing its support activities, links strategic sustainment to tactical combat service support. In MOOTW, the activities under operational support also pertain to support of US forces, other governmental agencies and forces of friendly countries or groups being supported by US forces.

OP.6.1 ARM OPERATIONAL FORCES
(JFLCC INTEREST)

H-97. To provide for the replenishment of arms, ammunition, and equipment required for supporting US Services and allied operational forces in conformance with operational commander's campaign or major OPLANs in addition to routine theater (or area) of operations consumption.

OP.6.2 PROVIDE
FUEL TO OPERATIONAL FORCES
(JFLCC INTEREST)

H-98. To provide for the uninterrupted flow of fuel (class III) of joint/multinational operational forces in conformance with the operational commander's campaign or major OPLANs in addition to routine theater consumption. The source-of-fuel system would include the inland, offshore, or any other fuel distribution system.

OP.6.3 FIX/MAINTAIN EQUIPMENT
(JFLCC INTEREST)

H-99. To provide for the establishment of facilities in the rear areas for the repair and replacement of materiel and the establishment of policies on repair and evacuation of equipment in support of operational forces in campaigns and major operations. This activity includes the concentration and provision of maintenance services, including recovery BDA and repair, and class IX supplies, for retaining operational forces in or restoring them to a high state of materiel readiness in preparation for sustaining the tempo of operations in campaign, major operations, and routine COMMZ support. This is largely a Service/national function.

OP.6.4 MAN OPERATIONAL FORCES
(JFLCC INTEREST)

H-100. To provide the uninterrupted flow of trained and organizationally sound units and replacements and to provide necessary personnel and health services support in the theater of operations for supporting campaigns, major operations, and routine COMMZ support. This is largely a Service/national function.

OP.6.4.1 PROVIDE FIELD, PERSONNEL,
AND HEALTH SERVICES
(JFLCC INTEREST)

H-101. To provide field services and supply and laboratory services (includes food, water, personal welfare and comfort items, clothing and individual equipment; laundry, bath, and renovation; and graves registration), personnel service support (includes administration, finance, chaplain, public affairs, legal services, and individual support activities), and health service support (includes medical C^4 intelligence, prevention, treatment and movement, hospitalization, return to duty, evacuation, veterinary and laboratory services, blood management, dental services, and combat stress control, medical threat intelligence) in preparing operational forces for campaigns, major operations, routine COMMZ support, and the sustainment of the tempo of operations once begun. This task includes providing rest and relaxation, rotation, and reconstitution guidance within an operational commander's responsibility. This is largely a Service/national function.

OP.6.4.2 RECONSTITUTE FORCES
(JFLCC INTEREST)

H-102. To take extraordinary actions to restore combat-attrited units to desired level of combat effectiveness commensurate with mission requirements and availability of resources. Reconstitution includes two types of activities: reorganization and regeneration. This is largely a Service/national function.

OP.6.4.3 TRAIN UNITS AND PERSONNEL
(JFLCC INFLUENCE)

H-103. To provide the means for training replacements and units, especially newly rebuilt units in the theater of operations. In MOOTW, this activity includes training assistance for friendly nations and groups. This is largely a Service/national function.

OP.6.4.4 CONDUCT
THEATER OF OPERATIONS
RECEPTION OPERATIONS
(JFLCC INTEREST)

H-104. To receive and prepare reinforcing units and individual replacements for further deployment and employment. Reception includes clearing airports of debarkation (APODs) and seaports of debarkation (SPODs), moving unit personnel and equipment from ports of debarkation to marshaling areas, joining unit personnel (normally deployed by air) with their equipment (normally shipped by sea or pre-positioned in storage sites or vessels), and providing supplies and support necessary to achieve readiness for onward movement. This is largely a Service/national function. Priorities should be influenced by the land force operational plan.

OP.6.4.5 PROVIDE PUBLIC AFFAIRS
IN THEATER AREA OF OPERATIONS
(JFLCC INFLUENCES)

H-105. To build and maintain the national will of the American public and our elected leadership to support military objectives through fair and balanced coverage by the American and international press. To advise the operational commander on public affairs operations that support or impact the warfighting scheme of maneuver. This task includes media relations, coordination, and escort of news media covering JFLC command forces; managing all tactical-level public affairs operations; and participating in the IO working group in support of the operational and strategic information campaign.

OP.6.5 DISTRIBUTE
(JFLCC INFLUENCES)

H-106. To maintain the timely flow of stocks (all classes of supply in large quantities) and services (maintenance and manpower) to operational forces, using joint or combined transportation means (over ground, air, and sea

LOCs) in support of campaigns and major operations and normal support operations. This is largely an Army/national function.

OP.6.5.1 PROVIDE MOVEMENT SERVICES (JFLCC INFLUENCES)

H-107. To move personnel, equipment, and supplies to sustain campaigns and major operations and to provide transportation resources for moving operational forces which execute those operations. This task includes transportation-mode operations, movement management and control, battlefield circulation control, and terminal operations. This is largely an Army/national function.

OP.6.5.2 SUPPLY OPERATIONAL FORCES (JFLCC INFLUENCES)

H-108. To provide trained manpower, all classes of supply, maps and water, and related services for sustaining operational forces throughout a campaign or major operation in the quantities and at the time and place needed. This task includes requesting, receiving, producing, procuring, storing, protecting (e.g., APODs, SPODs, log bases, etc.), relocating and issuing manpower, supplies, and services. It also includes building up the necessary stockage levels in staging areas for conducting the campaign. This is predominately a Service/national function.

OP.6.6 MAINTAIN SUSTAINMENT BASES (JFLCC INTEREST)

H-109. To build and maintain principal and supplementary bases for sustainment activities in conformance with theater-of-war commander's guidance. This is largely a Service/national function.

OP.6.6.1 RECOMMEND NUMBER AND LOCATION OF SUSTAINING BASES (JFLCC INTEREST)

H-110. To provide expertise to theater-of-war commander on lines of support and the suggested locations for sustaining bases so as best to support the operational commander's campaign or major OPLANs.

OP.6.6.2 PROVIDE
SUSTAINMENT ENGINEERING
(JFLCC INTEREST)

H-111. To dismantle fortifications and to construct and maintain facilities and communications networks that give physical structure to the LOCs, thus setting the capacity of combat service support organizations to provide materiel and services to operational commanders. This activity includes the following: building/maintaining forward staging bases, restoring rear area, sustaining LOC, supporting construction, and acquiring or producing construction material.

OP.6.6.3 PROVIDE
LAW ENFORCEMENT AND PRISONER CONTROL
(JFLCC INFLUENCES)

H-112. To provide, in the COMMZ and in support of the operational commander's campaigns and major operations, EPW collection processing, evacuation, internment; reporting and coordination with host nation, US staff agencies, and the International Red Cross. In addition, enforces military law and order and battle area circulation control.

OP.6.7 CONDUCT POLITICO-MILITARY
SUPPORT TO OTHER NATIONS, GROUPS,
AND GOVERNMENT AGENCIES
(JFLCC INFLUENCES)

H-113. To provide assistance in terms of personnel, materiel, and/or services (e.g., health services) that supports strategic and operational goals within the theater or AO. This task includes security assistance, civil-military operations support (e.g., humanitarian assistance, disaster relief, etc.), and other assistance from military forces to civilian authorities and population.

OP.6.7.1 CONDUCT SECURITY ASSISTANCE
IN THEATER (AND AREA) OF OPERATIONS
(JFLCC INTEREST)

H-114. To provide defense articles, military training, and other defense-related services to friendly nations or groups, by grant, loan, credit, or cash sales, in furtherance of national policies and objectives within a theater or AO.

OP.6.7.2 PROVIDE CIVIL-MILITARY OPERATIONS
SUPPORT IN THEATER (AND AREA) OF OPERATIONS
(JFLCC INFLUENCES)

H-115. To conduct activities in support of military operations in a theater or AO that embrace the relationship between the military forces and civilian authorities and population, and the development of favorable emotions, attitudes, or behavior in neutral, friendly, or hostile groups. Activities included in civil-military operations are civil affairs, military-civic action, humanitarian assistance (includes disaster relief), civil assistance, and PSYOP.

OP.6.7.3 PROVIDE SUPPORT TO DOD
AND OTHER GOVERNMENT AGENCIES
(JFLCC INTEREST)

H-116. To provide support of DOD, joint staff, other Services, civil governments, and other related agencies. This task could include, but is not limited to, supporting activities such as civil disturbances control, drug enforcement, combating terrorism, science and technology base, environmental protection, joint exercises, and operations.

OP.6.7.4 COORDINATE
POLITICO-MILITARY SUPPORT
(JFLCC INFLUENCES)

H-117. To be kept informed of and to coordinate activities among military commands, DOD, and other US governmental agencies, and friendly governments within the theater or AO.

OP.6.8 EVACUATE
NONCOMBATANTS FROM THEATER
(OR AREA) OF OPERATIONS
(JFLCC INTEREST)

H-118. To use theater of operations military and host-nation resources for evacuation of US military dependents, US government civilians, and private citizens (US and third nation). Organizations at various echelons provide support (medical, transportation, security, etc.) to the noncombatants; the support is analyzed under the appropriate activity. A large portion of this mission belongs to the Navy, although land forces would participate. Their participation, however, would probably be under their Service component commands. Use of theater land forces to conduct noncombatant evacuations would reduce the size of the JFLCC's forces.

OP 6.2.9 COORDINATE AND CONDUCT PERSONNEL RECOVERY (JFLCC INFLUENCES)

H-119. Provide for the support of isolated US military personnel and US civilians and other designated personnel within the theater of operations/JOA. This task includes reporting, locating, supporting the person and family, recovery and return of the isolated person to family or duty. The task further includes conducting civil and combat search and rescue missions and providing support to friendly personnel attempts of evasion and escape. To coordinate the use of aircraft, surface craft, submarines, specialized rescue teams and equipment, to include unconventional assisted recovery, for returning isolated personnel to US control. This task includes coordinating the locating, tracking, and reporting isolated or captured personnel.

Glossary

ABBREVIATIONS AND ACRONYMS

A^2C2	Army airspace command and control
AADC	area air defense commander
AAMDC	Army Air Missile Defense Command, area air missile defense commander
ADA	air defense artillery
ADCON	administrative control
AFFOR	Air Force forces
ALSA	Air Land Sea Application Center
AMD	air and missile defense
AO	area of operations
AOA	amphibious objective area
AOI	area of interest
APOD	airports of debarkation
ARFOR	Army forces
ASCC	Army Service component commander
AT	antiterrorism
ATACMS	Army Tactical Missile System
ATO	air tasking order
BCD	battlefield coordination detachment
BDA	battle damage assessment
C^2	command and control
C^2W	command and control warfare
C^4	command, control, communications, and computer
CA	combat assessment
CAB	combat assessment board

CAS	close air support
CCIR	commander's critical information requirements
CDE	chemical defense equipment
CFC	coalition force commander
CFLCC	coalition force land component command
CI	counterintelligence
CJCS	Chairman Joint Chiefs of Staff
CJTF	commander, joint task force
CMOC	civil-military operations center
COA	course of action
COCOM	combatant command (command authority)
COG	center of gravity
COMSEC	communications security
CONOPS	concept of operations
CONPLAN	concept plan
CTL	candidate target list
CUL	common user logistics
D³A	decide, detect, deliver, and assess
DAADC	deputy area air defense commander
DCA	defensive counterair
DIA	Defense Intelligence Agency
DOCC	deep operations coordination cell
DOD	Department of Defense
DTB	daily targeting board
EPW	enemy prisoners of war
EW	electronic warfare
FFCC	force fires coordination center
FSCM	fire support coordination measures
FSE	fire support element

HOC	HUMINT operations cell
HUMINT	human intelligence
ICW	in conjunction with
IO	information operations
ISB	intermediate support bases
ISR	intelligence, surveillance, reconnaissance
J-1	manpower and personnel directorate of a joint staff
J-2	intelligence directorate of a joint staff
J-2X	joint force J-2 CI/HUMINT staff element
J-3	operations directorate of a joint staff
J-4	logistics directorate of a joint staff
J-5	plans directorate of a joint staff
J-6	command, control, communications, and computer systems directorate of a joint staff
JACE	joint analysis and control element
JCMEC	joint captured materiel exploitation center
JDEC	joint document exploitation center
JFACC	joint force air component commander
JFC	joint force commander
JFLC	joint force land component
JFLCC	joint force land component commander
JFMCC	joint force maritime component commander
JFSOC	joint force special operations component
JFSOCC	joint force special operations component commander
JIDC	joint interrogation and debriefing center
JIF	joint interrogation facility
JOA	joint operations area
JOPES	Joint Operation Planning and Execution System
JP	joint pub
JPG	joint planning group

JSPS	joint strategic planning system
JTCB	joint targeting coordination board
JTF	joint task force
JTMD	joint theater missile defense
LCC	land component commander
LNO	liaison officer
LOC	lines of communication
MAGTF	Marine air-ground task force
MARFOR	Marine Corps forces
MEF	Marine expeditionary force
METT-T	mission, enemy, terrain and weather, troops and support available, and time available
METT-TC	mission, enemy, terrain and weather, troops and support available, time available, civilian
MNFC	multinational force commander
MOOTW	military operations other than war
MOPP	mission-oriented protective posture
MPAB	materials priorities allocation board
MSC	major subordinate command
NAVFOR	Navy forces
NBC	nuclear, biological, and chemical
NCA	National Command Authority
NGO	nongovernmental organizations
NIST	national intelligence support team
O&I	operations and intelligence
OGO	other governmental organizations
OPCON	operational control
OPLAN	operation plan
OPORD	operation order

OPSEC	operations security
PSYOP	psychological operations
PVO	private voluntary organizations
RFI	request for information
ROE	rules of engagement
SecDef	Secretary of Defense
SOF	special operations forces
SOP	standing operating procedure
SPOD	seaport of debarkation
SYSCON	systems control
TAAMCOORD	theater Army air and missile defense coordinator
TACAIR	tactical air
TACON	tactical control
TAMD	theater air and missile defense
TCB	targeting coordination board
TCS	Theater Communication System
TFCICA	task force counterintelligence coordinating authority
TMD	theater missile defense
TPFDD	time-phased force and deployment data
TST	time-sensitive target
UCP	Unified Command Plan
UNAAF	Unified Action Armed Forces
USA	United States Army
USCINCSOC	Commander in Chief, United States Special Operations Command
USMC	United States Marine Corps

TERMS AND DEFINITIONS

air interdiction   Air operations conducted to destroy, neutralize, or delay the enemy's military potential before it can be brought to bear effectively against friendly forces at such distance from friendly forces that detailed integration of each air mission with the fire and movement of friendly forces is not required. (JP 1-02)

amphibious objective area   A geographical area, delineated in the initiating directive, for purposes of command and control within which is located the objective(s) to be secured by the amphibious task force. This area must be of sufficient size to ensure accomplishment of the amphibious task force's mission and must provide sufficient area for conducting necessary sea, air, and land operations. (JP 1-02)

area air defense commander   Within a unified command, subordinate unified command, or joint task force, the commander will assign overall responsibility for air defense to a single commander. Normally, this will be the component commander with the preponderance of air defense capability and the command, control, and communications capability to plan and execute integrated air defense operations. Representation from the other components involved will be provided, as appropriate, to the area air defense commander's headquarters. Also called *AADC*. (JP 1-02)

area of operations   An operational area defined by the joint force commander for land and naval forces. Areas of operation do not typically encompass the entire operational area of the joint force commander, but should be large enough for component commanders to accomplish their missions and protect their forces. Also called *AO*. (JP 1-02)

battle damage assessment

The timely and accurate estimate of damage resulting from the application of military force, either lethal or nonlethal, against a predetermined objective. Battle damage assessment can be applied to the employment of all types of weapon systems (air, ground, naval, and special forces weapon systems) throughout the range of military operations. Battle damage assessment is primarily an intelligence responsibility with required inputs and coordination from the operators. Battle damage assessment is composed of physical damage assessment, functional damage assessment, and target system assessment. Also called *BDA*. (JP 1-02)

civil-military operations

Group of planned activities in support of military operations that enhances the relationship between the military forces and civilian authorities and population and which promote the development of favorable emotions, attitudes, or behavior in neutral, friendly, or hostile groups. (JP 1-02)

combatant command (command authority)

Nontransferable command authority established by Title 10 (Armed Forces), United States Code, section 164, exercised only by commanders of unified or specified combatant commands unless otherwise directed by the President or the Secretary of Defense. Combatant command (command authority) cannot be delegated and is the authority of a combatant commander to perform those functions of command over assigned forces involving organizing and employing commands and forces, assigning tasks, designating objectives, and giving authoritative direction over all aspects of military operations, joint training, and logistics necessary to accomplish the missions assigned to the command. Combatant command (command authority) should be exercised through the commanders of subordinate organizations. Normally this authority is exercised through subordinate joint force commanders and Service and/or functional component commanders. Combatant command (command authority) provides full authority to organize and employ commands and forces as the combatant commander considers necessary to accomplish assigned missions. Operational control is inherent in combatant command (command authority). Also called *COCOM*. (JP 1-02)

defensive counterair

All defensive measures designed to detect, identify, intercept, and destroy or negate enemy forces attempting to attack or penetrate the friendly air environment. Also called *DCA*. (JP 1-02)

fire support coordination line

A fire support coordination measure that is established and adjusted by appropriate land or amphibious force commanders within their boundaries in consultation with superior, subordinate, supporting, and affected commanders. Fire support coordination lines (FSCLs) facilitate the expeditious attack of surface targets of opportunity beyond the coordinating measure. An FSCL does not divide an area of operations by defining a boundary between close and deep operations or a zone for close air support. The FSCL applies to all fires of air, land, and sea-based weapon systems using any type of ammunition. Forces attacking targets beyond an FSCL must inform all affected commanders in sufficient time to allow necessary reaction to avoid fratricide. Supporting elements attacking targets beyond the FSCL must ensure that the attack will not produce adverse effects on, or to the rear of, the line. Short of an FSCL, all air-to-ground and surface-to-surface attack, operations are controlled by the appropriate land or amphibious force commander. The FSCL should follow well-defined terrain features. Coordination of attacks beyond the FSCL is especially critical to commanders of air, land, and special operations forces. In exceptional circumstances, the inability to conduct this coordination will not preclude the attack of targets beyond the FSCL. However, failure to do so may increase the risk of fratricide and could waste limited resources. Also called *FSCL*. (JP 1-02)

functional component command A command normally, but not necessarily, composed of forces of two or more military departments which may be established across the range of military operations to perform particular operational missions that may be of short duration or may extend over a period of time. (JP 1-02)

joint force air component commander The joint force air component commander derives authority from the joint force commander who has the authority to exercise operational control, assign missions, direct coordination among subordinate commanders, redirect and organize forces to ensure unity of effort in the accomplishment of the overall mission. The joint force commander will normally designate a joint force air component commander. The joint force air component commander's responsibilities will be assigned by the joint force commander (normally these would include, but not be limited to, planning, coordination, allocation, and tasking based on the joint force commander's apportionment decision). Using the joint force commander's guidance and authority, and in coordination with other Service component commanders and other assigned or supporting commanders, the joint force air component commander will recommend to the joint force commander apportionment of air sorties to various missions or geographic areas. Also called *JFACC*. (JP 1-02) (Note: The revised JP 3-0 will modify this term and definition.)

joint force commander   A general term applied to a combatant commander, subunified commander, or joint task force commander authorized to exercise combatant command (command authority) or operational control over a joint force. Also called *JFC*. (JP 1-02)

joint force land component commander   The commander within a unified command, subordinate unified command, or joint task force responsible to the establishing commander for making recommendations on the proper employment of land forces, planning and coordinating land operations, or accomplishing such operational missions as may be assigned. The joint force land component commander is given the authority necessary to accomplish missions and tasks assigned by the establishing commander. The joint force land component commander will normally be the commander with the preponderance of land forces and the requisite command and control capabilities. Also called *JFLCC*. (JP 1-02) (Note: The revised JP 3-0 will modify this term and definition.)

joint force maritime component commander The commander within a unified command, subordinate unified command, or joint task force responsible to the establishing commander for making recommendations on the proper employment of maritime forces and assets, planning and coordinating maritime operations, or accomplishing such operational missions as may be assigned. The joint force maritime component commander is given the authority necessary to accomplish missions and tasks assigned by the establishing commander. The joint force maritime component commander will normally be the commander with the preponderance of maritime forces and the requisite command and control capabilities. Also called *JFMCC*. (JP 1-02) (Note: The revised JP 3-0 will modify this term and definition.)

joint force special operations component commander The commander within a unified command, subordinate unified command, or joint task force responsible to the establishing commander for making recommendations on the proper employment of special operations forces and assets, planning and coordinating special operations, or accomplishing such operational missions as may be assigned. The joint force special operations component commander is given the authority necessary to accomplish missions and tasks assigned by the establishing commander. The joint force special operations component commander will normally be the commander with the preponderance of special operations forces and the requisite command and control capabilities. Also called *JFSOCC*. (JP 1-02) (Note: The revised JP 3-0 will modify this term and definition.)

joint operations area
An area of land, sea, and airspace, defined by a geographic combatant commander or subordinate unified commander, in which a joint force commander (normally a joint task force commander) conducts military operations to accomplish a specific mission. Joint operations areas are particularly useful when operations are limited in scope and geographic area or when operations are to be conducted on the boundaries between theaters. Also called *JOA*. (JP 1-02)

joint targeting coordination board
A group formed by the joint force commander to accomplish broad targeting oversight functions that may include but are not limited to coordinating targeting information, providing targeting guidance and priorities, and preparing and/or refining joint target lists. The board is normally comprised of representatives from the joint force staff, all components and, if required, component subordinate units. Also called *JTCB*. (JP 1-02)

joint task force
A joint force that is constituted and so designated by the Secretary of Defense, a combatant commander, a subunified commander, or an existing joint task force commander. Also called *JTF*. (JP 1-02)

Marine air-ground task force
The Marine Corps principal organization for all missions across the range of military operations, composed of forces task-organized under a single commander capable of responding rapidly to a contingency anywhere in the world. The types of forces in the MAGTF are functionally grouped into four core elements: a command element, an aviation combat element, a ground combat element, and a combat service support element. The four core elements are categories

of forces, not formal commands. The basic structure of the Marine air-ground task force never varies, though the number, size, and type of Marine Corps units comprising each of its four elements will always be mission dependent. The flexibility of the organizational structure allows for one or more subordinate MAFTFs, other Service, and/or foreign military forces to be assigned or attached. Also called *MAGTF*.

Marine expeditionary force The largest Marine air-ground task force and the Marine Corps principal warfighting organization, particularly for larger crises or contingencies. It is task-organized around a permanent command element and normally contains one or more Marine divisions, Marine aircraft wings, and Marine force service support groups. The Marine expeditionary force is capable of missions across the range of military operations, including amphibious assault and sustained operations ashore in any environment. It can operate from a sea base, a land base, or fboth. It may also contain other Service or foreign military forces assigned or attached to the MAGTF. Also called *MEF*. (JP 1-02)

operational control Transferable command authority that may be exercised by commanders at any echelon at or below the level of combatant command. Operational control is inherent in combatant command (command authority). Operational control may be delegated and is the authority to perform those functions of command over subordinate forces involving organizing and employing commands and forces, assigning tasks, designating objectives, and giving authoritative direction necessary to accomplish the mission. Operational control includes authoritative direction over all aspects of military operations and joint training necessary to accomplish missions assigned to the command. Operational control should be exercised through the commanders of subordinate organizations. Normally this authority is exercised through subordinate joint force commanders and Service and/or functional component commanders. Operational control normally provides full authority to organize commands and forces and to employ those forces as the commander in operational control considers necessary to accomplish assigned missions. Operational control does not, in and of itself, include authoritative direction for logistics or matters of administration, discipline, internal organization, or unit training. Also called *OPCON*. (JP 1-02)

Service component command
A command consisting of the Service component commander and all those Service forces, such as individuals, units, detachments, organizations, and installations under the command, including the support forces that have been assigned to a combatant command, or further assigned to a subordinate unified command or joint task force. (JP 1-02)

support
1. The action of a force which aids, protects, complements, or sustains another force in accordance with a directive requiring such action. 2. A unit which helps another unit in battle. Aviation, artillery, or naval gunfire may be used as a support for infantry. 3. A part of any unit held back at the beginning of an attack as a reserve. 4. An element of a command which assists, protects, or supplies other forces in combat. (JP 1-02)

supported commander The commander having primary responsibility for all aspects of a task assigned by the Joint Strategic Capabilities Plan or other joint operation planning authority. In the context of joint operation planning, this term refers to the commander who prepares operation plans or operation orders in response to requirements of the Chairman of the Joint Chiefs of Staff. (JP 1-02)

supporting commander A commander who provides augmentation forces or other support to a supported commander or who develops a supporting plan. Includes the designated combatant commands and Defense agencies as appropriate. (JP 1-02)

tactical control Command authority over assigned or attached forces or commands, or military capability or forces made available for tasking, that is limited to the detailed and, usually, local direction and control of movements or maneuvers necessary to accomplish missions or tasks assigned. Tactical control is inherent in operational control. Tactical control may be delegated to and exercised at any level at or below the level of combatant command. Also called *TACON*. (JP 1-02)

Bibliography

CJCSM 3122.01, *Joint Operation Planning and Execution System (JOPES)*. 14 July 2000.

JP 0-2, *Unified Action Armed Forces (UNAAF)*. 24 February 1995.

JP 1-02, *DOD Dictionary of Military and Associated Terms*. 10 June 1998.

JP 3-0, *Doctrine for Joint Operations*. 1 February 1995.

JP 3-01, *Doctrine for Countering Air and Missile Threats*. 19 October 1999.

JP 3-01.5, *Doctrine for Joint Theater Missile Defense*. 22 February 1996.

JP 3-02, *Joint Doctrine for Amphibious Operations*. 8 October 1992.

JP 3-03, *Doctrine for Joint Interdiction Operations*. 10 April 1997.

JP 3-07.2, *Joint Tactics, Techniques, and Procedures for Antiterrorism*. 17 March 1998.

JP 3-10, *Joint Doctrine for Rear Area Operations*. 28 May 1996.

JP 3-10.1, *Joint Tactics, Techniques, and Procedures for Base Defense*. 23 July 1996.

JP 3-11, *Joint Doctrine for Nuclear, Biological, and Chemical (NBC) Defense*. 11 July 2000.

JP 3-13, *Joint Doctrine for Information Operations*. 9 October 1998.

JP 3-16, *Joint Doctrine for Multinational Operations*. 5 April 2000.

JP 3-54, *Joint Doctrine for Operations Security*. 24 January 1997.

JP 3-55, *Reconnaissance, Surveillance, and Target Acquisition in Joint Operations*. 14 April 1993.

JP 3-60, *Doctrine for Joint Targeting* (draft). 5 April 2001.

JP 4-0, *Doctrine for Logistic Support in Joint Operations*. 6 April 2000.

JP 4-07, *Joint Doctrine, Techniques and Procedures for Common User Logistics* (draft). 28 December 2000.

JP 4-08, *Joint Doctrine for Logistic Support of Multinational Operations* (draft). 24 August 2000.

JP 5-00.2, *Joint Task Force Planning Guidance and Procedures.* 13 January 1999.

FM 3-50 (100-7), *Decision Force: The Army in Theater Operations* (draft). 1 October 2000.

FM 63-4, *Theater Support Command.* 24 September 1984.

FM 100-10, *Combat Service Support.* 3 October 1995.

ALSA *JTF Liaison Handbook.* August 1998.

By Order of the Secretary of the Army:

ERIC K. SHINSEKI
General, United States Army
Chief of Staff

Official:

JOEL B. HUDSON
Administrative Assistant to the
Secretary of the Army
0135303

DISTRIBUTION:
Active Army, Army National Guard, and U.S. Army Reserve: To be distributed
in accordance with the initial distribution number 115853, requirements for FM
3-31.

www.ingramcontent.com/pod-product-compliance
Lightning Source LLC
Chambersburg PA
CBHW060148300526
45790CB00014B/371